TECHNICAL
REPORT

T0302454

Data for DoD Manpower Policy Analysis

Jacob Alex Klerman

Prepared for the Office of the Secretary of Defense

Approved for public release; distribution unlimited

RAND NATIONAL DEFENSE RESEARCH INSTITUTE

The research described in this report was prepared for the Office of the Secretary of Defense (OSD). The research was conducted in the RAND National Defense Research Institute, a federally funded research and development center sponsored by the OSD, the Joint Staff, the Unified Combatant Commands, the Department of the Navy, the Marine Corps, the defense agencies, and the defense Intelligence Community under Contract W74V8H-06-C-0002.

Library of Congress Cataloging-in-Publication Data is available for this publication.

ISBN 978-0-8330-4208-8

Published 2009 by the RAND Corporation
1776 Main Street, P.O. Box 2138, Santa Monica, CA 90407-2138
1200 South Hayes Street, Arlington, VA 22202-5050
4570 Fifth Avenue, Suite 600, Pittsburgh, PA 15213-2665
RAND URL: http://www.rand.org/
To order RAND documents or to obtain additional information, contact
Distribution Services: Telephone: (310) 451-7002;
Fax: (310) 451-6915; Email: order@rand.org

Preface

This report presents a broad discussion of issues in data to support U.S. Department of Defense (DoD) manpower policy analysis. The report has two complementary audiences and two corresponding goals. First, with respect to the research community itself, the report outlines the available data and points out some underutilized data and some underutilized analytic strategies. Second, with respect to the DoD policy community, the review makes recommendations about how (and how not) to improve, refine, and expand the data-generation system.

This report was produced as part of the RAND project "Understanding Recent Trends in Veterans' Unemployment." That project seeks to understand the causes and consequences of unemployment among recently separated active-duty military personnel and reservists returning home from extended periods of active-duty service. As part of the effort for that project, the author organized a session, "The Effects of Military Service," at the July 2006 Western Economic Association Annual Meeting in San Diego and then an ad hoc "Workshop on Recent Veterans' Research" at RAND's Washington Office in December 2006. This document provides a more complete version of and justification for Klerman's remarks at those two meetings.

This research was conducted within the Forces and Resources Policy Center of the RAND National Defense Research Institute, a federally funded research and development center sponsored by the Office of the Secretary of Defense, the Joint Staff, the Unified Combatant Commands, the Department of the Navy, the Marine Corps, the defense agencies, and the defense Intelligence Community.

For more information on RAND's Forces and Resources Policy Center, contact the Director, James Hosek. He can be reached by email at James_Hosek@rand.org; by phone at 310-393-0411, extension 7183; or by mail at the RAND Corporation, 1776 Main Street, P.O. Box 2138, Santa Monica, CA 90407-2138. More information about RAND is available at http://www.rand.org.

Contents

Appendixes

Table

Summary

To allow analyses of its personnel practices, DoD maintains a multi-mode data collection effort. That effort includes both historical administrative data files and DoD surveys of military personnel. In addition, military manpower analyses make some use of civilian cross-sectional and longitudinal data.

This report considers this data collection effort as a system. For data users, it provides a high-level discussion of data strategies to support a variety of analytic goals. For data funders, it considers how the current system might or might not be expanded.

Beyond serving as a tutorial for analysts, the document has two main themes. The first theme concerns emerging, but currently underutilized, data-matching strategies. These strategies involving matching the core DoD administrative data files to (1) civilian administrative data (e.g., Social Security Administration earnings data); (2) DoD survey data; and (3) civilian survey data. Such data-matching initiatives raise important human subjects issues, but these issues can be addressed through interagency cooperation and appropriate research protocols. Recent experience suggests that the potential payoffs in better analysis for DoD—and therefore better policy—are large.

The second theme considers expanding the data collection effort. Specifically, DoD has been approached about participating in a National Longitudinal Survey of Youth for 2010 (NLS-Y2010) and about starting a military panel survey. Both of these efforts would be very expensive and, despite the expense, would have relatively small samples. With respect to an NLS-Y2010, if one is implemented, it will likely provide the data necessary for most military manpower analyses whether DoD participates or not. In addition, any such survey is likely to include so few people in the military as to be of minimal use in military manpower analyses. Thus, the incremental contribution of another wave does not seem to justify a large DoD financial contribution.

With respect to a DoD panel survey effort, this report concludes that the standard arguments for the utility of longitudinal surveys are incomplete. Many of the analytic advantages of longitudinal data can be achieved by analysis of repeated cross-sectional data. In addition, many of the research designs that such data could support can instead be supported—at lower cost and with larger samples—by creative matching of cross-sectional surveys and administrative data. Thus, funding for a DoD panel survey effort appears to lack a compelling research question that cannot be addressed by data matching.

Acknowledgments

This report was stimulated by the comments of Janice Laurence. Her direct and indirect impetus to write this document is much appreciated. At longer remove, this essay harkens back to the interests of Bernie Rostker. His role in the genesis of this document is gratefully acknowledged.

Some of the ideas developed here were initially conceived in preparation for a presentation at a session titled "The Effects of Military Service" at the July 2006 Western Economic Association International Annual Meeting in San Diego. David Chu and John Winkler provided the impetus for that session and my renewed systematic thinking about these issues. The comments of other participants in that session, Tom McClendon, Charles "Chick" Ciccolella, David Loughran, and Elaina Rose, helped to refine my thinking. These ideas were further developed in the context of the "Workshop on Recent Veterans' Research," held at RAND's Washington Office on December 11, 2006. Others whose comments improved this document include Craig Martin, Ben Karney, Nelson Lim, Paco Martorell, and James Hosek.

While I am grateful for the stimulating comments I have received, the opinions expressed here are my own. They do not necessarily represent the positions of those acknowledged, RAND, or its research sponsors.

Abbreviations

ACS	American Community Survey
ADPF	Active Duty Pay File
AFQT	Armed Forces Qualification Test
ASVAB	Armed Services Vocational Aptitude Battery
AVF	all-volunteer force
BLS	U.S. Bureau of Labor Statistics
CBS	choice-based sampling
CPS	Current Population Survey
DEERS	Defense Enrollment Eligibility Reporting System
DMDC	Defense Manpower Data Center
DoD	U.S. Department of Defense
DVA	U.S. Department of Veterans Affairs
GAO	U.S. Government Accountability Office
GWOT	global war on terrorism
ICR	Information Collection Request
LKM	Loughran, Klerman, and Martin (2006)
MEF	Master Earnings File
MEPCOM	Military Enlistment Processing Command
MOS	military occupational specialty
NLS	National Longitudinal Survey
NLS-Y2010	National Longitudinal Survey of Youth, 2010
NLS-Y79	National Longitudinal Survey of Youth, 1979
NLS-Y97	National Longitudinal Survey of Youth, 1997
NPS	non–prior service

OMB	U.S. Office of Management and Budget
OSD	Office of the Secretary of Defense
OUSD/P&R	Office of the Under Secretary of Defense for Personnel and Readiness
PSID	Panel Study of Income Dynamics
PTSD	post-traumatic stress disorder
RPF	Reserve Pay File
SIPP	Survey of Income and Program Participation
SOEP	Survey of Officer and Enlisted Personnel
SOFS	Status of Forces Surveys
SOFS-A	Status of Forces Survey of Active Component Members
SOFS-R	Status of Forces Survey of Reserve Component Members
SSA	Social Security Administration
SSN	Social Security number
WEX	Work Experience File
YATS	Youth Attitude Tracking Survey

CHAPTER ONE

Introduction

Background

The U.S. Department of Defense (DoD) is the nation's largest employer. Its employees play a vital role in homeland security and the advancement of U.S. foreign policy. To operate and improve DoD's manpower system, the department operates a large studies-and-research program. Its studies consider a range of issues. Among the most salient and recurring are recruiting new individuals into the uniformed military, retaining those individuals in the military, compensating those in the military, and providing support for families of those in the military. Underlying this large studies-and-research program is a large data-generation system.

This report presents a high-level and critical review of that data-generation system. The report has two complementary audiences and two corresponding goals. First, with respect to the research community itself, the report outlines the available data and points out some underutilized data and analytic strategies. Second, with respect to the DoD policy community, the report makes recommendations about how (and how not) to improve, refine, and expand the data-generation system.

The discussion is structured around the two-dimensional typology of data sources shown in Table 1.1. Along the columns, we have military-specific data versus civilian data (however, note that "civilian" data often include at least some military personnel). Along the rows, we have administrative data and two types of survey data. The two types of survey data are distinguished by whether the same people are interviewed once (cross-sectional survey data) or reinterviewed multiple times (longitudinal or panel survey data). The cells list the most salient data sources corresponding to each row and column. The list is not exhaustive.

Table 1.1
Typology of Data Sources and Leading Examples

Data Sources	Military-Specific Data	U.S. Population Data
Administrative	Work Experience File (WEX), Active Duty Pay File (ADPF), Reserve Pay File (RPF), Military Enlistment Processing Command (MEPCOM) files, Defense Enrollment Eligibility Reporting System (DEERS)	Social Security Administration Master Earnings File (SSA MEF), U.S. Department of Veterans Affairs (DVA)
Cross-sectional survey	Survey of Officer and Enlisted Personnel (SOEP), Status of Forces Survey of Active Component/ Reserve Component Members (SOFS-A and SOFS-R)	Decennial Census, American Community Survey (ACS), Current Population Survey (CPS)
Longitudinal (panel) survey	(Millennium Cohort Study)	National Longitudinal Survey of Youth, 1979 and 1997 (NLS-Y79 and NLS-Y97)

In the case of the military, some of this data-generation system is a product of the operational systems for managing the force (i.e., almost all the administrative data); however, some of that system exists solely for research and other forms of policy analysis (i.e., almost all the survey data). A similar relation exists on the civilian side. In general, administrative data are generated for administrative purposes and available for research as a side benefit. In contrast, survey data are collected almost exclusively for research.

Organization of This Report

The rest of this report is organized into nine chapters that reconsider this data-generation system. Chapters Two, Three, Six, and Seven consider, respectively, military administrative data, military cross-sectional surveys, civilian cross-sectional survey data, and civilian panel data. Chapters Four and Five consider matching across types of data. Chapters Eight and Nine consider major extensions to the current military survey effort. Chapter Eight considers a deeper cross-sectional effort, while Chapter Nine considers a military panel survey, and assumes that any such survey would include the "deeper survey" approach of Chapter Eight. Chapter Ten concludes with a summary of the main points and a repetition of the paper's recommendations to DoD and the Defense Manpower Data Center (DMDC).

Appendix A presents a more formal and technical discussion of some of the issues discussed in the body of the report. Appendix B provides the verbatim Census language about how residences are classified for military personnel, and Appendix C provides the exact wording of questions about military service in the major Census Bureau survey efforts.

CHAPTER TWO

Military Administrative Data

The uniformed services have millions of members. It is difficult to imagine how such a personnel system operated in the period before computers. Certainly, what we think of today as military manpower policy analysis using individual-level data was not feasible. However, for several decades, DoD has managed and paid its workforce—active, reserve, and civilian—using computerized systems. These computerized administrative data have made possible much of what we think of today as military manpower policy analysis.

Around the same time that computerization made these analyses possible, a crucial shift in manpower policy sharply increased the need for such analyses. Through the early 1970s, the United States operated a draft: DoD could and did simply require young people to enlist. Then, in 1973, the nation shifted to an all-volunteer force (AVF), which meant that DoD needed to induce young people to enlist voluntarily. This shift to the AVF, in turn, led to a need to better understand the decision to enlist, the decision to reenlist, and how these decisions are affected by compensation, family, and DoD policies.

Today, DoD constructs and keeps current these administrative data systems for the day-to-day operation of the military. They are crucial in answering a number of key questions: What are the available forces? Where are they? How much need they be paid? Who are in their families and thus eligible for dependent benefits?

Current Main Administrative Data Systems

DMDC maintains historical versions of its administrative files for analysis (and sometimes also for operational) purposes. Originally established in 1974, DMDC today is a part of the DoD Defense Human Resources Activity. DMDC's primary role is to support "the information management needs of the Office of the Under Secretary of Defense for Personnel and Readiness (OUSD/P&R)" (DMDC, 2006). Specifically, DMDC collects and maintains an archive of manpower, personnel, training, and financial databases for DoD. From these databases, DMDC provides analysis files, specific tabulations, and broad analyses for OUSD/P&R and other military analysts in DoD and in the broader research community.[1]

The 2006 *DMDC Profile* lists dozens of administrative files. However, as Stafford (1986) notes with respect to civilian labor market analyses, research focuses on a much narrower set of files. In our experience, the key files include the Work Experience File (WEX); the Military

[1] This discussion is based on the 2002 *DMDC Profile*. The 2006 edition is available at authorized personnel on the RAND Web site (DMDC, 2006).

Enlistment Processing Command (MEPCOM) files; the Active Duty Pay File and Reserve Pay File (ADPF and RPF); and the Contingency Files. Here we provide a brief description of each of these administrative data files.

WEX/Work Experience File. The WEX contains a longitudinal record for each individual who has served in the active or reserve forces since September 1990. For those individuals, the WEX includes information on service back to 1975. People who were not in the force after September 1990 do not appear in the file. The file is organized by "transactions"; in other words, a new record is generated whenever there is a change in the key variables—service/component/reserve category, pay grade, occupation (primary, secondary, or duty), and unit identification code. For 1993 forward, the underlying data are monthly. For earlier years, the underlying data range from quarterly to annual.[2]

The WEX is built from information in DMDC's Active Duty Master Personnel Edit File (AMPEF), equivalent reserve files, and the underlying service files. For many purposes, the WEX replaces those files and the files derived from them, providing a single longitudinal all-service, officer/enlisted, active/reserve file. For other purposes, the underlying files have key data components not available in the WEX. Analysts must consult the *DMDC Profile* (DMDC, 2006) and consult with DMDC file managers.

MEPCOM/Military Enlistment Processing Command. This file contains one record for every enlisted application for military service, regardless of whether it resulted in an accession. If an individual applied multiple times, there will be multiple records. Details vary by year, but at least since 1988, this files contains additional individual information as of application: Armed Forces Qualification Test (AFQT) results, age, education, height, weight, other medical conditions, and waivers. Officers are not included in the MEPCOM data. One major deficiency of MEPCOM data is that they do not include any information on enlistment incentives (bonuses, college fund benefits, and loan repayment). This information (usually service-specific) is recorded in other data files and can (perhaps easily) be appended to the MEPCOM file. Cash bonuses actually received are recorded (with a lag) in the pay files (see the next paragraph). More broadly, for analysis, information on bonuses and other terms of service offered (beyond any package actually taken) is crucial, but appears not to be recorded anywhere.

ADPF and RPF/Active Duty Pay File and Reserve Pay File. The ADPF and RPF contain detailed monthly (in early years, quarterly) active and reserve pay information (back to 1993 and 1997, respectively); however, the data from 1993 through 1995 appear to be incomplete or missing (see especially ADPF of January 1995 and December 1993).

Contingency Files. Information on actual deployment can be found in a sequence of "contingency files." The most recent of them is the Global War on Terrorism (GWOT) Contingency File. It contains one record for every activation or deployment in support of GWOT. Unfortunately, the contingency files for other contingencies (e.g., Sinai, Bosnia) do not appear to be complete or current.

---

[2] It should be noted that the WEX is not the official personnel file for the services (e.g., with respect to authorized end strength). Actual counts from the WEX will differ from official counts (usually by only a small amount).

Limitations of Administrative Data Systems

These files are, appropriately, the foundation of most military manpower analyses. They cover the entire universe, not a sample.[3] Inasmuch as these data are used for decisions, they will often be of high quality (or at least of higher quality than survey data the same topic). However, as we discuss below, they are far from perfect.

Administrative data vary widely in their quality. Any analyst who has worked with administrative data has horror stories. Variables are "unpopulated" (i.e., missing) totally, or for some years, or for some subpopulations. Even when data are present, they are sometimes nonsensical (e.g., not valid values), inconsistent across years, or simply implausible. The general rule of thumb is that information used for decisions is likely to be of higher quality[4] (e.g., Hotz et al., 1998). In general, the more frequent and important the decision, the higher the quality of the data. Thus, pay data are likely to be of relatively high quality. (If people are underpaid, they complain; auditing is intended to find people who are overpaid.)

At the other extreme, consider information on civilian education in military data. Information about civilian education is crucial for accessions. The fraction of accessions who are high school graduates is considered to be a key "quality" measure. High school nongraduates are required to have higher AFQT scores. Those with some minimal level of college can sometimes enter the military at a higher grade (and, therefore, pay). Recruiters are expected to obtain formal documentation of claimed educational attainment. We would, therefore, expect data on education at accession to be of relatively high quality.

In contrast, military files often have information on current education level. The quality of this data is suspect. There is no clear process of updating educational attainment, and personnel themselves have no incentive to do so. Few military pay rates or benefits appear to vary with civilian education once individuals are in the service. Consistent with this perspective, this variable is almost always identical to the accession education variable from which it is drawn. For this reason, at a 2006 public meeting, a senior DMDC official discouraged analysts from using these variables.

Analyses by Karney and Crown (2007) appear to have found similar issues with respect to marital status. DoD needs to record marital status, because it affects military pay (e.g., Basic Allowance for Housing [BAH]) and benefits (e.g., the qualification of spouses for health insurance through the Civilian Health and Medical Program of the Uniformed Services [CHAMPUS]). This information is collected at the RAPIDS station when the military sponsor presents appropriate documentation (e.g., a marriage certificate or a divorce decree) to the verifying official. The data are then transferred to the Defense Enrollment Eligibility Report-

---

[3] In the early years of military manpower policy analysis, computer power to analyze full files was a challenge. Today—beyond the initial exploratory phase—computer power is rarely an issue. Analysis of full files is the rule.

[4] This general rule is subject to an important caveat. Consider the example of administrative data on welfare payments. Administrative data on payments are likely to be of high quality. In many cases, one can argue that the administrative data define (or nearly define) the correct answer. In contrast, survey responses will often be far from that correct answer (e.g., Brady and Luks, 1995, on welfare receipt). Similarly, information on how the payment was computed is also likely to be of high quality. More precisely, the information is likely to be what was used in computing the appropriate payment.

Whether the information is actually correct is more complicated. Sometimes, however, the fact that the information will be used as part of the administrative process itself leads to biases. For example, welfare recipients have an incentive to underreport their earnings. Doing so increases their welfare payment. Consistent with the likely bias suggested by this incentive, Hill et al.'s 1997 comparison of state welfare records with tax return data found that (self-reported) state welfare data understate the earnings of welfare recipients.

ing System (DEERS) system. Marital status changes do appear to be recorded, eventually. However, the data appear to show bunching, as though marriage and divorce are not recorded in real time. Examination of recent data for the Navy Reserve suggests that, on activation, reservists were asked to review their recorded spousal information. Not surprisingly, the data show a spike in changes in marital status (especially divorce) at activation. Some of that spike may be real (e.g., a surge of divorces just before deployment), but much of it is probably because of the recording of previously unrecorded changes that had accumulated over years. Similarly, DMDC and the Army suspect that a widely noted jump in reported divorce rates in 2004 was primarily the result of how the Army handled a conversion to a new data system.[5]

Data processing issues can also induce problems in administrative data. Any change in the process that involves entering information into the administrative data system is likely to introduce artifacts into the data. For example, in the early 2000s, DoD followed federal information policy and shifted from one coding of race/ethnicity to a different coding. Across the shift, race/ethnicity data are not comparable. Furthermore, the shift appears to have occurred at different times in different services and even at different times within a given service. This is true even though all the data are recorded in the single MEPCOM database, a joint (i.e., cross-service) effort.

These examples emphasize that "administrative data" collected by a contemporaneous process (rather than a retrospective survey) require standard data cleaning work and, ultimately, caution in their use. In survey data, we know that changes in survey instrument will induce shifts in the time series without any change in underlying behavior. Sometimes, seemingly appropriate survey data will turn out not to be useful. The same will be true in administrative data. DMDC file managers know their files well and therefore tend to know a lot about these issues.

Recommendations for Improving the Utility of DMDC Administrative Data

Unfortunately, information about the content and quality of DMDC administrative data is only imperfectly conveyed to the user community. New mechanisms (e.g., some form of searchable blog, wiki, or other Internet resource) might help with this dissemination challenge.

Another idea would be to set up a DMDC-sponsored email discussion group for the community using each data file. DMDC staff could participate in discussions as appropriate. It seems likely that DMDC is reluctant to have its staff make public statements about the data without formal clearance. An email discussion group would encourage communication without requiring DMDC leadership to clear public statements of staff. Some organizations proceed by explicitly stating that remarks made by employees in such email discussions do not reflect the official policy of the employing organization. With that explicit caveat, it may be possible to allow employees to participate slightly more actively in such discussions without consuming inordinate amounts of management time (and delaying responses) for the screening of staff postings. The proper balance between these considerations and, thus, the nature of DMDC participation in such an email discussion is an issue for DMDC management.

In conclusion, the incremental cost to DoD of making these administrative data available for policy analysis is small relative to the cost of fielding survey efforts of similar sample size.

---

[5] Conversations with DMDC staff.

DMDC performs that role well. Our only other recommendation is that DMDC give more resources to ensuring the proper archiving of historical data. A simple scan of the previous list of files reveals that many of the historical series do not go back much before the turn of the millennium, and a few not even that far.

Archiving is an ongoing challenge for all data archives. Because archiving is such a challenge, several institutes in the social sciences (e.g., the Inter-University Consortium for Political and Social Research) aim to archive collected data. DMDC is urged to review its procedures and to benchmark them against best practices in other agencies (e.g., the U.S. Census Bureau, the U.S. Bureau of Labor Statistics [BLS]).

CHAPTER THREE

Current Military Cross-Sectional Survey Programs

The administrative data discussed in the previous chapter include *much* of the objective information about military service. However, they do not include *all* the information needed for policy analysis. Specifically, the administrative data include no subjective information about military service, nor any information on what happens outside the military (e.g., spousal earnings, intentions, marital satisfaction, child outcomes, and mental health[1]).

Surveys are the standard way to collect such information. In this chapter, we consider the current DoD cross-sectional survey effort and possible incremental changes to it. Later, in Chapters Eight and Nine, we sketch two different models for the DoD survey effort that might complement the existing military cross-sectional survey effort.

Current Cross-Sectional Survey Programs

Consider first the current survey program. Since 1969, DMDC has fielded a set of surveys of the uniformed population (often referred to as the "Survey of Officer and Enlisted Personnel"). Large surveys were conducted in 1978, 1985–1986, 1991–1992, and 1999–2000. Details vary by year, but these surveys included active and reserve personnel and their spouses (and matched pairs of service person and spouse are available for the 1985–1986 and 1991–1992 surveys).

Beginning in 2002, these surveys were replaced by a number of survey programs at DMDC. Web administration (with postal and email notifications) is used for Status of Forces Surveys (SOFS) of service members and DoD civilian employees. These surveys are currently administered three times per year to active duty members, twice per year to reserve members, and once per year to civilian DoD employees.Spouses of active-duty and reserve members are surveyed via the Web with a paper survey option as part of the Human Relations Survey Program. These surveys were done in 2005–2006 and are planned for 2007–2008. In 2007, DMDC began experimenting with QuickCompass polls of service members and their spouses, as well as DoD civilian employees. Experiments are being conducted to see whether any of these populations, in whole or in part, can be quickly polled on the Web using only email notifications and reminders.

[1] The new Post-Deployment Health Assessment attempts to collect mental health information (including a proxy for post-traumatic stress disorder [PTSD]). However, as its name suggests, it is administered only to those returning from deployment. Neither baseline information for those who deploy nor information on those who do not deploy appears to be available.

Similar to the design of many national surveys, each SOFS questionnaire asks fixed questions and questions that vary cyclically or to fit a specific survey time period. That is, SOFS have three components: (1) core items included in every survey of that population, (2) cyclical coverage of items per the OUSD/P&R-approved content plan, and (3) topical questions that vary with current DoD policy issues.

The topical section's content varies. For example, May 2004 questions of the reserve components included questions on income change, the demobilization process, and reemployment after deactivation. Concern about apparent elevated rates of unemployment income receipt led to questions about unemployment income receipt and plans for employment on exit in the May 2006 survey.

Limitations of Current Cross-Sectional Survey Efforts

These surveys are appropriately a key component of DoD/DMDC's data collection strategy. The shift to a thrice-yearly frequency provides DoD with timelier information on all measures and the ability to specify new questions to address emerging issues. It is crucial, however, to understand the limitations of the DoD/DMDC survey effort.[2] Here we consider several of those limitations: (1) sample size, (2) differential nonresponse, (3) response error, and (4) survey concept. We defer until Chapters Eight and Nine to discuss two other limitations of the current DoD survey effort: (5) the relative shallowness of information collected on each individual and (6) the lack of longitudinal information.

Sample Size

DMDC's survey efforts are among the largest survey efforts anywhere. Standard sample sizes are in the tens of thousands; the May 2004 SOFS reserve survey sampled more than 55,000 people. However, these surveys are still administered to far less than the entire population. The incomplete coverage results from two interrelated factors. First, the basics of sampling theory suggest that it is possible to infer information about the whole population from a properly constructed sample (see Bregger, 1984); so, it is not necessary to contact everyone. Of course, sampling is also much, much cheaper than surveying the entire population. However, once we sample, the number of cases for relatively uncommon subgroups declines rapidly. This is in contrast to administrative data, which usually include everyone.

Intelligent stratified sampling can partially address the lack of sample in rare, but important, subgroups. Such stratified sampling is particularly easy for surveying the military. The personnel records provide a rich sampling frame from which individuals in target groups can be identified at minimal cost. DMDC follows this approach and over-samples some subgroups. Nevertheless, sample size remains a disadvantage of surveys relative to administrative data.

The second reason that DMDC surveys do not include the entire population is that not everyone in the sample (i.e., selected to receive a survey) actually responds. Nonresponse is a feature common to all surveys. However, more intensive—longer and more expensive—survey methods yield higher response rates. DMDC's surveys use among the least expensive survey methods. Originally fielded as mail-out/mail-back surveys, today they are usually administered using a Web-based form for response.

---

[2] For a similar discussion, see Hotz et al., (1998, Chapter Four).

An additional factor lowering response rates to the SOFS is that the field period for the surveys is quite short—about six weeks from first possible response to the close of the survey period. This short fielding period is consistent with the SOFS effort's role in providing current information about the force. However, this short field period also has negative implications. Civilian survey research finds that the longer the fielding period, the higher the response rates (DMDC, 2007d). The short response period is likely to be especially problematic for military surveys. The nature of military service—especially military service since September 11, 2001—has been that of frequent and long deployments, more intensive training, and longer workdays, even for those not training or deployed who are nevertheless covering for those who are training or deployed. Some training and deployed service persons have no access to email or regular mail through which to receive the notices. Others receive mail, but have only limited access to the Web to respond. Even those with the necessary connections are likely to be quite busy and stressed (Hosek, Kavanaugh, and Miller, 2006). Responding to a survey may not be the highest priority for their time. Such stress may only be temporary. Nonetheless, six weeks is a short time relative to the time required to prepare, perform, and recover from a training exercise or deployment. However, DMDC internal analyses suggest that there would be little gain from extending the fielding period.

Despite these concerns, the SOFS response rates are better than what would be expected from civilian surveys using similar methods. Nevertheless, they are quite low—in the range of 30 to 40 percent (e.g., 36.3 percent for the May 2005 Status of Forces Survey of Reserve Component Members [SOFS-R]).

Differential Nonresponse

If sample size is the only consideration, these inexpensive methods are appropriate. Even with their low response rates, these field methods have much lower costs per completed case than do the alternatives. Costs for these methods are very roughly $10 per completed case. Costs for the next more intensive option—a phone survey—would be very roughly $50 per completed case. Costs for the most expensive option—in-person interviews—would be very roughly $250 per completed case. Although these are very rough estimates, they still reflect huge differences in cost per completed case.

Simple sample size, however, is *not* the only consideration. Sampling theory suggests that surveys deliver approximately the same results as a complete enumeration, under one crucial condition: The sample of respondents must be randomly selected from the universe.

However, when response rates are well below 100 percent, respondents are likely to differ from nonrespondents. Simple algebra (see Appendix A) and conventional wisdom suggest that the lower response rates are, the more likely there are to be differences between respondents and nonrespondents; such differences can cause survey-based estimates—which can only be based on the responses of respondents—to diverge from the true answers in the population as a whole, which includes both respondents and nonrespondents.[3]

At what level low response rates become problematic is a subject of considerable controversy in the survey research community. In addition, it is an area in which the consensus appears to be shifting. To understand the controversy, note that, almost by definition, differential nonresponse is difficult to identify. If we had good data on differential nonre-

---

[3] But see Groves (2006), who emphasizes that under some circumstances higher response rates can actually lead to larger bias. That case seems unlikely in general and especially in the case of the SOFS, given its quite low response rates.

sponse, we would use that data to re-weight. Comparing the gross observable characteristics of respondents to the administrative data's characterization of the universe (and the population selected for the sample), we know that there is considerable differential nonresponse. However, DMDC has already used (much of) that information to re-weight. The re-weighting eliminated any bias from differential nonresponse according to any *observable* characteristics used in the re-weighting.

The problem is with differential response with respect to unobserved characteristics. We cannot re-weight for them, and we also cannot know that any bias exists. (This last statement is too strong, but it conveys the nature of the problem.) In the literature, there are at least two approaches to evaluating the magnitude of nonresponse bias (e.g., Groves, 1989, 2006). Some of these methods also work with conventional survey response error (see below).

The first approach is to use more-intensive field methods on some subsample of the nonresponses. One would then compare the characteristics of responses using the less-intensive methods with the characteristics of responses using the more-intensive methods.[4] DMDC has conducted tests of the effect of more intensive mail follow-up. Those tests suggest that the additional cost and field period does not yield a large change in the resulting estimates (DMDC, 2007e; Caplan, 2003). Furthermore, they note that differential nonresponse is less important in their surveys than in general population surveys. General population surveys have limited information on nonrespondent. In contrast, DMDC's surveys are list-based. DMDC therefore has much better information about the characteristics of nonrespondents. They can and do use that information in constructing weights to adjust for differential nonresponse.

The second approach is to match the original sample to some external information. Again, one then compares the characteristics of respondents to those of nonrespondents according to this external information. Martorell, Klerman, and Loughran (2008) do this for the 2005 and 2006 SOFS-R. Specifically, with the cooperation of DMDC and the Social Security Administration (SSA), they compare military pay and Medicare earnings histories as recorded in SSA administrative data across survey respondents and nonrespondents. They have found that neither civilian earnings nor military pay varies substantially between (weighted) survey respondents and the entire population.

Both of these results are consistent with there being little bias from differential nonresponse in DMDC's Status of Forces Surveys program. However, the evidence is limited. There is a much larger literature in the broader domain of survey research, and the consensus there appears to be shifting. Conventionally, survey nonresponse was assumed to be differential. Considerable efforts were often invested in intensive survey methods to achieve "high" response rates. An oral wisdom based on (and reflected in) a series of U.S. Government Accountability Office (GAO) documents gave target response rates in the range of 70–80 percent (see Groves, 2006, for several versions of this oral wisdom). The 2006 U.S. Office of Management and Budget (OMB) guidance calls out 80 percent as a goal. The actual OMB language is as follows (OMB, 2006a, p. 61):

---

[4] See Kessler, Little, and Groves (1995) for a vivid example of this approach. In a survey of the prevalence of psychiatric disorders, members of a small subsample of nonrespondents were offered $1,000 to answer a very limited mental health screening battery. Consistent with the worst fears of survey researchers, these responding nonrespondents had a much higher prevalence of mental illness. In this case, nonresponse was clearly biasing the results. Kessler, Little, and Groves (1995) discuss how large the implied bias truly is. They argue that the nonrespondent group was small enough that even though they were different from the respondents, the effect on overall means was small.

> ICRs [Information Collection Requests to OMB] for surveys with expected response rates lower than 80 percent need complete descriptions of how the expected response rate was determined, a detailed description of steps that will be taken to maximize the response rate . . . and a description of plans to evaluate nonresponse bias. . . . Agencies also need a clear justification as to why the expected response rate is adequate based on the purpose of the study and the type of information that will be collected (whether influential or not). This discussion may include past experience with response rates when studying this population, prior investigations of nonresponse bias, plans to evaluate nonresponse bias, and plans to use survey methods that follow best practices that are demonstrated to achieve good response rates.

Conversations with OMB leadership suggest that this 80 percent rule is arbitrary.

Furthermore, the OMB guidance is explicit in stating that, while some methods are likely to yield lower response rates, the method chosen does not justify a lower response rate (OMB, 2006). The exact language is as follows (OMB, 2006a, p. 62):

> Different modes of data collection typically yield differences in response rates, depending on the target population and specific methods used. For example, while a 60 percent response rate to a mail survey or RDD [random-digit-dial] telephone survey may be considered quite good for some populations, such a response rate would not be considered as good for a personal visit survey. However, there are not established differences in risk for nonresponse bias by mode that would suggest that a 60 percent response rate in one mode carries a higher risk of nonresponse bias than another mode. Therefore, OMB has not set different thresholds . . . for different data collection modes.
>
> Agencies need to consider how the choice of data collection mode will affect their response rates, potential for nonresponse bias, and the information that will be available to assess potential nonresponse bias . . . and weigh these factors along with the other advantages and disadvantages of the modes or modes of collection they are considering. Agencies need to justify in their ICRs their choice of mode given the advantages and disadvantages of that mode.

In considering the implications of this OMB best-practice guideline for DMDC's survey efforts, we note that OMB's target response rate of 80 percent is approximately twice the level that DMDC is achieving in its surveys in the mid-2000s.

It is important to note, however, that this OMB guidance may, for three reasons, be obsolete. The first reason is that (as OMB acknowledges) survey response rates appear to be dropping rapidly. The marquee federal survey efforts themselves (e.g., Current Population Survey, [CPS], Survey of Income and Program Participation [SIPP], and National Health Interview Survey [NHIS]) are often only barely getting 80 percent response rates, and then only with in-person interviews. For other nonmarquee (and not as well-funded) survey efforts, response rates of 80 percent appear to be nearly unattainable, certainly without extraordinary expenditures.

Second, in the survey community, a revisionist perspective has argued that nonresponse bias is much less severe than had previously been believed (Keeter et al., 2000; Kessler, Little, and Groves, 1995). See Groves (2006) for a sensitive review of that literature and a reasoned set of implications. The discussion below draws partially on his conclusions.

Martorell, Klerman, and Loughran's (2008) analysis of earnings of activated reservists is consistent with this revisionist perspective. They match the sample for the SOFS-R—

respondents and nonrespondents—to SSA earnings data. They find that respondents and nonrespondents differ, but that reweighting eliminates much of the difference. Thus, this analysis provides additional support for the conjecture that with proper weighting, nonresponse bias need not be a major concern.

Third, with modern computer technology, it is much easier to design mixed-mode survey methods (e.g., Kessler, Little, and Groves, 1995; Groves, 2006; Groves et al., 2005). Such mixed-mode survey methods allow for the use of cheaper methods (with much lower response rates) for most cases and more expensive methods (with much higher response rates) for a limited subsample. Results from the two samples can be compared in real time. If and when evidence of a discrepancy emerges, resources can be shifted toward the more intensive method. This is a real-time version of the suggestion above to "use more intensive field methods on some subsample of the non-responses."

Finally, we note that the OMB guidance is arguably less applicable to DMDC survey efforts. Conventionally, the OMB guidance applies to general-population surveys, in which little is known about nonrespondents. DMDC surveys of the military are based on list samples. We know a lot about both respondents and nonrespondents: specifically, anything in the administrative data (e.g., gender, race/ethnicity, age, service, rank, education, and AFQT score at entrance). This rich list data allows DMDC to construct much richer weighting schemes than is possible in a simple population survey in which nothing is known about nonrespondents beyond the most basic characteristics of the population as a whole (e.g., gender, race/ethnicity, age, perhaps education). While this argument has considerable validity, it is our understanding that OMB holds both general-population surveys and list surveys (for which better weights could be constructed) to the same standard.

Response Error

Returning to our initial list of limitations of survey data, we consider response error. Survey data are only as good as the quality of the responses. For some subjective questions, the truth is whatever the respondent answers. For objective questions, survey responses may not always line up with the objective information that the survey was intended to collect. Information about earnings and anything requiring recall are often particularly problematic (on response errors, see Biemer et al., 1991).

Specifically in the military survey context, Martorell, Klerman, and Loughran (2008) are also informative for the broader issue of response error. By comparing SOFS-R data to military pay records, Martorell, Klerman, and Loughran show quite clearly that survey respondents underreport their military earnings. These results are consistent with civilian survey evidence that earnings information is reported with considerable error (Weinberg et al., 1999; Angrist and Krueger, 2001). The problem appears to be worse for this population because respondents are not clear on what "earnings" concept the survey is asking about.

Survey Concept

We conclude our discussion of issues with survey data with an amorphous concern about survey concept. As the modern literature on survey methods emphasizes, survey data collection is a complicated interpersonal interaction between interviewer (or form) and respondent (e.g., Biemer et al., 1991). Respondents answer the question they thought they were asked. Unfortunately, how respondents interpret a question is rarely clear. Thus, what income concept will a respondent use when asked about annual income? Will they include "special pays"? Will they include military "allowances"? Will they include the value of the special tax treatment of some military earnings?

Survey designers attempt to address this problem by including additional wording in the questions and supplemental text when they think the respondent may be unsure how to answer. However, the respondent will not always request (or read) the supplemental text. Sometimes, a respondent will misinterpret or ignore the text of the question. For example, a recent SOFS question rewording to clarify the period over which average monthly earnings were to be given appears to have been interpreted by some respondents as requesting annual earnings (see Loughran, Klerman, and Martin, 2006). The question wording is not ambiguous. However, when read quickly (or partially heard), it is not hard to imagine that response errors would be induced. In fact, response errors appear to be common, limiting the utility of the responses. The importance of this phenomenon will vary with the domain being explored. Income and earnings appear to be particularly problematic.

CHAPTER FOUR

Matching DoD Administrative Data to DoD Cross-Sectional Surveys

Having discussed two types of data—military administrative data and military cross-sectional survey data—we are ready to consider one of the themes of this report—matching. Our discussion of military administrative data and military survey data has emphasized that the two types of data are complementary, each having its advantages and disadvantages.

Examples of Matching DoD Administrative to Cross-Sectional Surveys

The two types of data—administrative and survey—need not be distinct. DMDC's survey operations already use administrative data to draw their survey samples and to do nonresponse follow-up. Similar linkage of survey data to administrative data could be used to enhance analysis. For example, James Hosek at RAND is exploring the effect of a variety of factors (e.g., whether deployment was longer than expected, number of times the service member worked longer than the usual duty day in the past year, and whether the service member felt prepared and felt his or her unit was prepared, as well as actual deployment) on reenlistment. In earlier analyses of SOFS-A data, Hosek, Kavanaugh, and Miller (2006) found that a high frequency of long duty-days among service members are very strongly correlated with reenlistment *intentions*. Other work suggests that intentions are correlated with actual reenlistment (Orvis, 1992). To explore later reenlistment choices, Hosek is matching the earlier survey data to DMDC administrative data on personnel files (from which one can infer reenlistment decisions).

Note the structure of this analysis. The survey data alone are not sufficient. They do not include detailed information on service (patterns of deployment, receipt of bonuses) or prospective information on choices. The administrative data alone are also not sufficient. They do not have information on deployment expectations, hours worked, or the frequency of long duty-days. However, given that DMDC knows the Social Security number (SSN) corresponding to each completed survey, it is, in principle, possible to match the earlier survey data to later administrative data.

Issues in Matching DoD Administrative Data to Cross-Sectional Surveys

Such analyses—matching survey responses to the corresponding administrative data—are feasible. They are also potentially problematic. DMDC promises confidentiality to its survey respondents and rightly guards these data to guarantee that confidentiality. It does so in part by subjecting all such matching to formal human subjects review—first at the home institution and then at DMDC.

These safeguards are appropriate. From an ethical perspective, promises of confidentiality must be respected. From an instrumental perspective, any breach of those promises would severely and negatively affect the DMDC survey effort. Researchers simply need to build into their project plans sufficient time and budget to satisfy the legitimate human subjects concerns.

Suggestions for Dealing with Issues in Matching DoD Administrative Data to Cross-Sectional Surveys

The potential for matched survey-administrative data analyses seems so great that DMDC is urged to explore a range of approaches for providing access to restricted data. For instance, the University of Michigan's Data Sharing for Demographic Research Project has explored these issues.[1]

For DMDC, one approach worthy of further consideration would be to establish a "cold room." Any analysts using the cold room would be required to sign a nondisclosure agreement and be subject to penalties for violating the agreement. Within the cold room, analysts could do any type of analysis (including looking at individual records). However, no results of such analyses could leave the cold room unless they were explicitly reviewed for possible violation of confidentiality.[2]

---

[1] The Data Sharing for Demographic Research Project's Web site contains some information (Data Sharing for Demographic Research, undated), and its staff provides consulting services.

[2] This is the procedure that the U.S. Census Bureau uses in its Research Data Centers (U.S. Census Bureau, undated). The National Center for Health Statistics has recently concluded an agreement allowing its sensitive data to be used in the Census Research Data Centers. It seems plausible that DMDC could conclude a similar agreement.

CHAPTER FIVE

Matching DoD Administrative Data to Civilian Administrative Data

Outside of DoD, federal and state governments also maintain administrative data systems for operating nonmilitary government programs. In addition, they archive historical versions of those data. Such data include information on annual earnings from the SSA, information on quarterly earnings and receipt of unemployment insurance from state unemployment insurance programs, information on health care utilization in federal and state Medicaid and Medicare records, and information on use of veterans' benefits from the Department of Veterans Affairs.

The earlier methodological review of survey data suggests that, where available, such administrative data are likely to have much larger samples and to be of considerably higher quality than corresponding survey data. For a similar discussion of the role of administrative data in civilian policy analysis, see Hotz et al. (1998).

Alone, these civilian administrative data are of limited use to military manpower analysts. Our primary interest is in outcomes for specific individuals—e.g., current reservists, spouses of current service persons, and veterans (but see the discussion of potential uses in the next chapter). These individuals are not usually so identified in these administrative data. However, most of those systems include an SSN. It is thus, in principle, possible to match military administrative data to these civilian administrative data. As such, these administrative data files are potentially of considerable value to military manpower research.

Examples of Matching DoD Administrative Data to Civilian Administrative Data

In an early series of papers, Goldberg and Warner (1987), Angrist (1990, 1998), and Angrist and Krueger (1994) used matched DMDC and SSA data to explore the effect of military service on civilian earnings for various cohorts of veterans. More recently, Loughran, Klerman, and Martin (2006; hereafter "LKM") have matched SSA earnings data to DMDC data to explore earnings loss of activated reservists. DMDC survey data suggest that earnings loss is common. However, identifying activated reservists using DMDC administrative data and their earnings (civilian and military) from a combination of SSA data and DMDC administrative data, LKM find that most reservists have large gains and that losses are relatively rare. Furthermore, LKM argue that the administrative data are likely to be of higher quality.

This methodology appears to be quite promising. Loughran and Klerman are extending this methodology to earnings after return from active duty and to the effect of activation and deployment on spousal earnings. In the absence of such administrative data, the conventional approach to imputing civilian earnings in retention studies has been to use all "similar" civilians, where "similar" was defined in terms of a limited set of covariates—gender, race/ethnicity, age, education, and perhaps occupation. With SSA earnings data, we can impute earnings based on actual earnings of those who left in the previous year.

Issues in Matching DoD Administrative Data to Civilian Administrative Data

Again, issues of confidentiality arise, both for the DoD administrative data and for the non-DoD administrative data. On a formal level, DMDC has negotiated data-sharing agreements with many of the natural data partners. In the case of SSA data, SSA maintains a sort of "super–cold room" arrangement. Researchers submit data to be matched to SSA earnings data, along with programs to do analyses on the matched data. SSA runs the programs, verifies that the results satisfy confidentiality criteria, and then returns the results to the analyst. The analyst never sees individual records. This approach has worked quite well for LKM.

This approach has two important limitations related to the information actually in administrative data. Administrative data often include only an identifier (e.g., an SSN and perhaps also some combination of name, address, and date of birth) and the key administrative outcome (e.g., for the SSA, earnings). Thus, the first limitation is that it is often not possible to form useful "comparison groups." We may be able to identify service persons (by linking based on the SSNs), but we often cannot identify people "like" service persons. Some administrative data (e.g., state unemployment insurance program data) do not even have data on age or gender. Information on education (and certainly AFQT score) is almost always absent. Service persons are a very selected sample. Simply comparing their outcomes to those of the entire population (e.g., for the SSA data, workers) is unlikely to provide useful comparisons.

This problem is partially remediable if we have SSNs for a comparison group. For example, if we want to analyze the effects of military service, applicants for military service are a natural comparison group (Angrist, 1998), and their SSNs are recorded in their MEPCOM applicant records (even though they never enlisted). DMDC has those MEPCOM files. It is thus possible for military manpower analysts to identify those individuals in SSA earnings data. It is crucial to note that analysts never have access to true SSNs: not from DMDC, not from SSA, and not from any other data provider. Instead, DMDC provides analysts with data that includes only pseudo-SSNs: DMDC provides SSA or other data providers with a "link file" associating the pseudo-SSNs with the true SSNs. SSA uses this link file to match the DMDC data to the other data. Analysts have no need to know the true SSNs, and, with this procedure, they never learn them.

Second, beyond the inability to identify useful comparison groups, the administrative data often do not have the outcomes of interest. For example, while information on earnings is useful, earnings might be low because the individual was in school—but the administrative data usually will not record school attendance. Similarly, for some purposes, *total* earnings is a useful concept, whereas for other purposes, hourly earnings is a more useful concept. But again, the administrative data often do not have information on hours worked, so it is not possible to infer an hourly wage.

Suggestions for Dealing with Issues in Matching DoD Administrative Data to Civilian Administrative Data

One approach to remedying these problems with missing data is to analyze survey data. Survey data often collect a wider range of information about respondents (albeit for a much smaller sample and with lower data quality). The next chapter therefore considers matching DoD administrative data to civilian survey data.

CHAPTER SIX

Matching DoD Administrative Data to Civilian Cross-Sectional Surveys

The previous three chapters considered DoD survey data and matching DoD administrative data to DoD survey data and civilian administrative data. This chapter considers the uses of civilian data for military manpower analysis and the possibility of matching DoD administrative data to civilian survey data.

Current Civilian Cross-Sectional Surveys

The U.S. Census Bureau runs numerous surveys of the general population. These surveys include information on place of residence, family structure (e.g., marital status, presence of children), education (attainment and current attendance), unemployment, employment, earnings, and other sources of income. These civilian surveys have three leading uses in military manpower policy analysis:

- **Population at Risk:** For analyses of recruiting, the population at risk (i.e., those who might enter) is some subset of civilians. To understand who is more likely to enlist, we need information on the prevalence of characteristics among enlistees and in the youth population as a whole (or better, those who would have been eligible to enlist). For examples of such studies, see Hosek and Peterson (1985, 1990).
- **Alternatives:** For those considering enlistment, enlisting is a choice between life in the military and a civilian life. To understand those civilian options, military manpower analyses need information on outcomes for civilians "similar to" those who did enlist. Similarly, for those in the military, retention is a choice between staying in the military and exiting to the private sector. Again, to understand those civilian options, military manpower analysts need information on civilian outcomes (or better, on civilian outcomes for those who leave the military). For studies of this form, see Asch, Kilburn, and Klerman (1999).
- **Comparison Groups:** Sometimes, military manpower questions concern the extent to which military outcomes differ from civilian outcomes. Thus, for example, several studies (Hosek et al., 2002; Harrell et al., 2004; and Lim, Golinelli, and Cho, 2007) have examined whether military spouses earn less than otherwise similar civilians.

In civilian labor market analyses and in these military manpower analyses, civilian survey data has been a traditional source for such information.[1] Three of these civilian surveys are particularly relevant for military manpower analysis.

- **Decennial Census:** The decennial Census attempts to collect information on every American. For approximately one in every 20 Americans, the Census long form includes more detailed information on employment, earnings, and other outcomes than the basic (short) Census form. The samples are thus huge, but there is relatively little information on each individual, and there are large gaps (10 years) between surveys. Changes to the Census imply that much less information will be available from the 2010 Census.[2]
- **Current Population Survey:** The CPS is a monthly survey of about 50,000 households.[3] The survey's primary purpose is to provide the official unemployment rate. It also includes some questions about veteran status. The U.S. Department of Labor uses this information to construct a separate (but noisy) measure of unemployment for young veterans. In addition, in March of each year, the CPS's Annual Social and Economic Supplement includes more information about employment and earnings. In some years (April 1985; November 1987; September 1989, 1991, and 1993; August 1995; and September 1997, 1999, 2001, 2003, 2005, and 2007), the CPS has also included a special Veterans Supplement as part of the survey.
- **American Community Survey (ACS):** The ACS is a new (since 2000) Census Bureau survey that asks CPS-like questions of about 250,000 households each month. This is approximately 3 million households a year (i.e., nearly 3 percent of the entire U.S. population). It is intended to be intermediate between the decennial Census and the CPS—a survey of relatively large size that is administered every month.

Each of these surveys collects a broad range of information, including household structure and, for each member of the household, basic demographics (gender, age, relationship to head of household, and education) and labor market information (employment and hours worked). Often, these studies also collect information on school attendance, hourly wages, total earnings, and total income.

Issues in Using Civilian Surveys for Military Manpower Analyses

This is a much broader set of items than is available in most administrative data sets. As noted, these surveys are used regularly in military manpower analyses. Nevertheless, military manpower analyses that use these data face three challenges: sample size, sampling frame, and identifying service persons.

---

[1] See Angrist and Krueger (2001, S3.1, p. 1332f) for a useful overview of civilian data sets. We will see below that alternative data sources for civilian information might sometimes be preferable.

[2] Specifically, the Census short form includes only minimal information for creating congressional districts—age, gender, and race/ethnicity. More detailed information is contained on the long form. However, with the 2010 Census, a combination of the American Community Survey and administrative records is projected to replace the Long Form.

[3] The CPS is not a simple repeated cross-sectional survey. Dwelling units are surveyed for four consecutive months in two consecutive years. This panel is relatively short (at most 15 months), and the CPS is usually analyzed as a cross-section (ignoring the potential correlation), thus the classification of the CPS here.

Sample Size

With respect to sample size, the crucial issue is that, while DoD is the nation's largest employer, the number of people in the military is relatively small. Military personnel represent slightly less than 1 percent of the nation's population. Even including their immediate families (spouses and children), they represent less than 2 percent of the nation's population. Thus, even very large surveys of the general population will have relatively few members of the military or their families. From this perspective, the CPS's 50,000 households is probably too small. That sample is likely to include well under 500 military families. These considerations are less salient in the huge Census and ACS surveys.[4]

Sampling Frame

Analysts using civilian surveys to analyze military populations need to be quite careful about the sampling frame. Some surveys consider only the resident population; service persons serving overseas are not included. Similarly, some surveys consider only the civilian noninstitutional population; some service persons (and sometimes their spouses living on base) are not included in the survey sampling frame. For example, the CPS is a survey of the U.S. resident civilian noninstitutionalized population. Therefore, military personnel living in barracks or overseas are not included (Lim, Golinelli, and Cho, 2007). It appears that military personnel living off base are in the sample frame. The treatment of those living on base in nonbarracks housing is unclear. Appendix B provides the 2000 Census rules.

Identifying Service Persons

Even when the individuals are sampled and sample sizes are large enough, identifying those currently or ever in the military is a challenge; correlating outcomes with the details of military service (e.g., dates of service, active versus reserve, military occupation, experience of combat) is nearly impossible. Appendix C gives the exact question battery. In brief, the March CPS file has a simple battery of questions: It asks whether the respondent is a veteran, during which period he or she served, and whether the respondent is now in the armed services. The 2000 Census and the ACS also ask whether someone was in the reserves and whether he or she served more than two years on active duty. This is limited information. Clearly, using this information alone, it is not possible to relate subsequent civilian outcomes to the details of military service (e.g., occupation, component, grade, service overseas, combat). In fact, for many policy issues, the survey questions are maddeningly incomplete (e.g., was this person a member of the active component or an activated reservist?). Interagency working groups are currently moving to expand some of these questions to include more detail about active versus reserve and about service in GWOT. However, even after these questions are expanded, information on respondents' military careers will be quite limited.

Matching DoD Administrative Data to Civilian Cross-Sectional Surveys

Again, an alternative strategy involving matching appears to be possible. The CPS asks people to supply their SSNs and asks permission to impute SSNs for those who do not provide one.

[4] See Lim, Golinelli, and Cho (2007) for a sample size analysis for using multiple years of the CPS to analyze employment patterns of military spouses.

The Census and the ACS request SSNs. For those who do not provide an SSN, one is imputed based on name.[5] Thus, it should be possible to match DMDC administrative data to Census Bureau survey data. The Census Bureau makes such analyses of merged data possible through its Research Data Center program. For example, Ringel and Klerman (2005) merged California welfare data with CPS data on program participation to understand reporting error in the CPS.

In fact, the U.S. Census Bureau is quite interested in such analyses. In an attempt to minimize the response burden of its surveys, it is actively exploring matching to administrative data (Prevost, 2006). Matching to DoD administrative data (for a fee) is likely to be possible and of considerable interest to the Census Bureau. However, such matches do not appear to have been done (or even attempted).

[5] Response to the Census and ACS is mandatory; people may choose not give an SSN, but they cannot prevent the Census Bureau from imputing an SSN.

CHAPTER SEVEN

Civilian Panel Surveys and Choice-Based Sampling

The previous chapter considered civilian *cross-sectional* surveys. In this chapter, we consider the utility of civilian *panel* (sometimes called *longitudinal*) surveys for military manpower analysis. These surveys follow the same individuals over time. We begin with an overview of what is, from the perspective of a military manpower data analyst, the most useful of these surveys: the National Longitudinal Survey (NLS) effort.[1] We then discuss the issues of sample size and choice-based sampling as a response. Finally, we consider the utility of over-sampling service personnel.

The National Longitudinal Survey Effort

For our purposes, the NLS is a sequence of panels of people. Four panels were begun in the late 1960s, including a panel of young men and a panel of young women. Youth panels were begun in 1979 (the NLS-Y79) and 1997 (the NLS-Y97).[2] Another youth panel has been proposed to start in 2010 (see Pierret, 2006).

For the NLS-Y79 and NLS-Y97 efforts, DoD has been a significant partner to the Department of Labor, the lead department. The main use of these data in manpower analysis has been for recruiting policy. First and most important, the 1979 and 1997 data on nationally representative youth populations were used to renorm the Armed Services Vocational Aptitude Battery/Armed Forces Qualification Test (ASVAB/AFQT).

Second, the data have been used to improve our understanding of the enlistment decision. Enlistment is a choice made by civilians. From MEPCOM data, we know a great deal about enlistees. However, to understand enlistment, we also need to understand those individuals who did not enlist. They are not in the MEPCOM data. Instead, we need information on the entire civilian population. It is, therefore, not surprising that these data have been intensively used to study recruiting and enlistment (Antel, Hosek, and Peterson, 1987; Hosek and Peterson, 1990). Some analyses have used civilian repeated cross-sectional surveys such as the University of Michigan's "Monitoring the Future" study (see the discussion in Orvis, 1992).

1 The NLS efforts are most useful because they begin with a cohort of young people. Other surveys begin with a cross-section of the general population. Military service and, in particular, enlistment are concentrated among the young. General panel surveys have too few young people to study the youth population, and only a handful of people in the military.

Another possibility would be the U.S. Department of Education's National Educational Longitudinal Survey (NELS). That survey appears to have been little used in military manpower analyses.

2 For more information on the NLS effort, see U.S. Department of Labor (undated).

Others have used DoD's Youth Poll and its predecessor, the Youth Attitude Tracking Survey (YATS; again, see Orvis, 1992).

Another strategy is to use panel data to follow a cohort of young people forward. The analyst observes everyone's characteristics and attitudes. In addition, the analyst observes who enlists. From this information, the analyst can compute the probability of enlistment given certain characteristics.

Sample Size Issues and Choice-Based Sampling

How useful are civilian panel surveys for following outcomes for a military population? In practice, this analysis strategy faces a serious barrier: sample size. We truly have panel data only if we successfully interview a very high proportion of the sample (or at least those who answered the first interview) in every period. This reality forces panel data surveys to use much more intensive survey methods, often in-person interviews. As a result, response rates are higher and data quality appears to be better. However, because of the high cost per case, sample sizes are small, well under 15,000. The expected number of enlistees is well under 1,000. Recent analyses of GWOT service in the NLS-Y97 had only 393 people who had even served in the military—across all four services, active and reserve, including both those with successful military careers and those who "washed out" of basic training (Black and Lane, 2007). Since most of the NLS-Y97 sample is past the prime enlistment ages, that number will grow only slightly as the panel matures.

This is simply not enough cases to do most analyses, especially once we note the heterogeneity of the underlying population. For example, addressing concern about labor market outcomes of recent veterans, Black and Lane (2007) try to build an analysis on the 173 people reporting an exit from the military at some point during the panel. Even this population included many reservists (the exact breakdown is unclear from their analysis). Furthermore, they report high noninterview rates for those with military experience, speculating that these high noninterview rates may be the result of deployment. Plausibly, they find that unemployment shrinks rapidly with time since separation. This is a substantively important result because it helps to explain why unemployment is higher among young veterans than among their nonveteran counterparts. Nevertheless, this attempt to analyze the initially unemployed separately is based on only 35 individuals. Any attempt to stratify this population—unfortunately, even active versus reserve—is likely to be futile.

The problem here is not some flaw in the design of the NLS-Y97. Military service is simply not common among today's youth. Any moderate-sized population sample will include only small numbers of people with any military service. Inasmuch as the sample is being drawn from youth below the age of military service, as is the pattern for the NLS-Y effort, it will not be possible to over-sample those in the military.[3] Over-sampling at entrance to the military loses much of the power of the longitudinal design: prospectively collected preenlistment information. The only solution appears to be taking a much larger sample, but that option appears to be fiscally infeasible in the current environment. Any follow-on NLS-Y effort at all (e.g., an NLS-Y2010) seems far from certain.

[3] See below for a discussion of deliberately over-sampling those in the military.

One potentially promising approach is choice-based sampling (CBS). Under CBS, a sample is constructed by combining civilian records from the survey with military records, for different people, from administrative data. On CBS in general, see Amemiya (1985). On CBS in the military context, see Hosek (1979) and Hosek and Peterson (1983). With CBS, both the civilian and military samples can be quite large.

One possible choice-based sample could be created by pairing the NLS-Y and MEPCOM data. For this strategy to be effective, the ASVAB scores in the MEPCOM data would need to be comparable to the ASVAB scores in the NLS-Y data. However, there are two crucial differences between the ASVAB scores from each data source. First, in the MEPCOM data, the ASVAB is a high-stakes test: The results of the test have a direct, immediate, and large consequence, as they can determine whether the individual is allowed to enlist. In contrast, in the NLS-Y, the ASVAB is a no-consequence test. The second important difference is that the NLS-Y97 respondents took the ASVAB in their mid-teens, whereas most MEPCOM files have their subjects' ASVAB scores as of about age 20. There is some attempt at age standardization, but it is not clear whether that standardization is sufficient.

Unpublished analyses of the NLS-Y97 by Klerman provide some insight into the comparability of ASVAB scores. Those analyses find that, as measured by MEPCOM ASVAB scores, DoD policy keeps the fraction of category IVs (respondents who scored in the 16th to 30th percentile from the bottom on the Armed Forces Qualifying Test) in the military extremely low (under 1 percent in this period). In contrast, among NLS-Y97 sample members who are recorded as entering the military, between 5 and 10 percent of enlistees are category IVs. Three plausible pathways might explain this result: (1) the NLS-Y97 sample took the ASVAB in their mid-teens—perhaps ASVAB scores from tests administered when the respondent is younger are poor proxies for scores from tests administered when the respondent is older;[4] (2) scores on high-stakes tests are higher than scores on no-consequence tests; and (3) scores vary across multiple tests. Limited exploration of these issues suggests that (1) and (2) are likely to be important.

Administrative data such as the MEPCOM files are unlikely to have all of the desired information. An alternative approach is to match MEPCOM data to a special-purpose cross-sectional survey and then to analyze that data combined with civilian panel data using CBS methods. However, to use this strategy, we would need to verify that cross-sectional survey data can reproduce what would have been collected with the NLS-Y97's annual in-person data collection strategy. Some recall or method effects are inevitable (Groves, 1989; Tourangeau, Rips, and Rasinski, 2000). How large they would be is unclear.

The cross-sectional nature of such a survey raises other issues. It is likely to catch only part of the NLS-Y's cohort sample. Are such cohort effects important? In many cases, the answer is likely to be "yes." The business cycle, military requirements, and, most recently, overseas conflict would be expected to shift who enlists across periods.

These are open questions. They need to be answered on an analysis-by-analysis basis. For some analyses, a special cross-sectional survey will be plausible and, perhaps, attractive; for other analyses, it will not be.

---

[4] The NLS-Y97 renormalizes the test by age (for three-month age groups), so the issue is not the levels. Rather, the issue is the stability of the percentile rankings across ages.

A Military Over-Sample

One approach to these small sample sizes would be to over-sample those in the military; in other words, at the same time that the initial survey sample is drawn, also draw a sample of people in the military. Give both samples the same questionnaire and follow them forward.

The NLS-Y79 included such an over-sample. That survey drew an initial survey of young people age 14 to 21.[5] That initial sample was drawn by "screening" civilian households (i.e., interviewers knocked on a random sample of addresses and asked whether anyone 14 to 21 lived at that address). This approach would have missed people already in the military, so the NLS-Y drew a sample of people in the military.

Given the need to a draw a small sample already in the military to make the main sample representative of all young people 14 to 21, it was relatively easy for the NLS-Y effort to increase the size of the military sample. DoD paid for them to do so. In total, 1,793 people already in the military were sampled according to a stratified sampling scheme that over-sampled women and clustered the sample in units. Of them, 1,280 (72 percent) responded to the first interview. Few analyses appear to have used those data. Presumably, this was the reason that DoD did not continue paying to follow this subsample, which was last interviewed in 1985.

DoD Participation in an NLS-Y2010

DoD has now been approached about partnering in the follow-on NLS-Y2010.[6] That survey is projected to select a sample of 8,000 to 12,000 individuals age 12 to 17. They would then be followed and reinterviewed annually.

Unless the NLS-Y2010 is much larger than currently projected (which seems unlikely) or military enlistment increases sharply (which seems even less likely), the projected number of participating enlistees for the NLS-Y2010 is likely to be about 500. As was just noted, this is simply too small to do serious analysis of the enlistment decision. Thus, concerns about sample size for enlistment analyses are likely to remain.

Again, one approach would be to over-sample those in the military. However, given the limited use of the NLS-Y79 over-sample, an over-sample for NLS-Y2010 does not seem promising. Furthermore, actually implementing an over-sample would be more difficult for an NLS-Y2010 than it was for the NLS-Y79. The NLS-Y2010 is projected to sample individuals 12 to 17. None of those people are yet in the military. Thus, an over-sample will require going back

---

5 See U.S. Department of Labor (2004).

6 In considering participation in any NLS-Y2010 effort, it is important to note that BLS's plans appear to involve much larger financial contributions by "partner" agencies. Pierret (2006) states,

> In the current fiscal environment, it is difficult for a single Federal agency to secure the funding necessary to start a new cohort. . . . BLS has always provided the great majority of the funding. . . . Interagency funding typically has paid for the marginal costs of specific survey questions or special activities related to the research objectives of other agencies. Under a consortium approach, BLS will share both the survey design and funding responsibilities more evenly with other agencies.

This language appears to apply weaker BLS support for an NLS-Y2010 effort than was true for earlier NLS-Y panels. Whether such an effort will actually occur—beginning in 2010 or in some year shortly thereafter—seems far from certain. It seems unwise for DoD to plan data collection strategies based on the assumption that such a survey will actually occur (unless, of course, DoD decides that it is willing to shoulder a major fraction of the costs).

several years later and drawing a new sample as members of this cohort enter the military. Prime enlistment ages are 18 to 20, so such an over-sample would need to be drawn two to eight years after the initial sample was drawn.

What about other uses of an NLS-Y2010 for military manpower analysis? Another national panel of youth should be useful in recruiting analyses, both to better understand the youth population and for analyses using CBS. However, such analyses do not appear to require DoD participation in the NLS effort. Any NLS-Y2010 effort would need to collect information on family background and military enlistment. That is all that is needed to do recruiting analyses. Perhaps DoD might fund collection of slightly more detail on service careers (e.g., component, military occupational specialty [MOS], rank).[7]

The NLS-Y efforts have been particularly useful for manpower analyses, because they have included the ASVAB/AFQT results. DoD used the NLS-Y79 and NLS-Y97 samples to renorm the ASVAB results. Such renorming requires a random sample of the youth population, and the NLS effort provided one. The drift in the norms between 1979 and 1997 suggests that another renorming in 2010 might be useful (e.g., continued immigration, changes in education).

Note, however, that the NLS-Y2010 is projected again to interview younger people. DoD needs to know the distribution of ASVAB scores in the prime recruiting population (e.g., ages 18 to 20). The correlation between early and late ASVAB scores is high, but far from perfect. This limits the utility of the NLS-Y ASVAB for military policy analysis. Perhaps DoD should fund the NLS-Y2010 to re-administer the ASVAB as the cohort turns 18.

The ASVAB scores are also useful for analysis. What are people in the prime recruiting population (e.g., category IIIAs—those who scored in the 50th to 64th percentiles from the bottom on the Armed Forces Qualifying Test) doing? How many of them go to college? These ASVAB/AFQT variables have also been very powerful for civilian research. It therefore seems likely that the NLS-Y2010 would include the ASVAB results even if DoD did not fund it. Perhaps in the absence of DoD funding, the NLS-Y2010 would adopt some alternative test. Arguments of continuity across the waves of the NLS would suggest not.

---

[7] Note, however, that other data strategies allow similar analyses. For example, subsequent DoD administrative data (i.e., MEPCOM data) explore the relationship between family background factors, propensity, and enlistment using YATS matched to enlistment data (Warner, Simon, and Payne, 2003).

CHAPTER EIGHT

An Alternative Model for Military Cross-Sectional Surveys

Chapter Three described the current DMDC cross-sectional survey effort, critiqued it, and suggested some possible incremental changes. In this chapter, we consider a very different type of military cross-sectional survey.

DMDC's Current Survey Effort

DMDC's current survey effort collects limited information on very large samples. This is similar to the Census Bureau's strategy with respect to the ACS. Often in conjunction with a longitudinal component (discussed in the previous chapter), some civilian surveys have gone in a very different direction. Such surveys have collected detailed information on a limited set of individuals—both through the survey itself and through adjunct data collection efforts. For example, recent NLSs have collected not only interview information on demographics and labor market experience, but also ASVAB scores, height and weight, and detailed school transcripts. Furthermore, spouses and children of the primary sample members have also been surveyed. Other major civilian panel surveys (e.g., the Panel Study of Income Dynamics [PSID], the Health and Retirement Survey [HRS]) have also been augmented by complementary data collection efforts.

DoD does not currently take this approach. The cross-sectional survey efforts stand alone. When there is a special data collection need, a new sample is created (e.g., Hosek's survey of deployment experiences; Hosek, Kavanaugh, and Miller, 2006) or a supplement is added (e.g., in the SOFS). Alternatively, information is collected on the entire population (e.g., the Post-Deployment Health Assessment), but this information is not linked back to DMDC survey files.

An Alternative Model

DoD and DMDC might consider creating a second survey effort. That survey effort would have a much smaller sample, but DMDC might make a deliberate effort to collect much richer information on the sampled members. Such efforts might include (1) surveying people multiple times (i.e., a panel survey; see the next chapter); (2) surveying not only the service person, but also any spouse or children, and, in the case of reservists, employers; (3) appending administrative data from MEPCOM and WEX; (4) appending information on use of DoD services (e.g., child care and health care); (5) appending information on psychological assessments; and (6) conducting a much longer survey (e.g., on attitudes toward services and marital satisfaction).

Such an effort raises at least three issues. First, it would be more expensive. Whether the benefits justify the costs is an open issue. Second, there are important confidentiality issues. The more information that is matched to the files, the easier it would be for someone—especially someone with access to the administrative data files—to identify the survey respondents. Third, such an intensive effort would impose significant burdens on the respondent. Some form of compensation (e.g., a cash payment of $100 per interview) or release time would need to be considered.

CHAPTER NINE

A Military Panel Survey

Returning to the typology of Table 1.1 in Chapter One, we have considered five of the six cells. With a partial exception that we discuss at the end of this section, the sixth cell is empty: There is not currently a military panel survey. We begin this chapter by considering two arguments against a military panel survey: cost and the incremental contribution of surveys given the existing availability of administrative data. We then turn to two arguments in favor of a military survey: truly longitudinal analysis and better controls for unobservables. Finally, we discuss some design issues for such a military panel survey.

This order—first disadvantages and then advantages—deliberately reverses the standard presentation. While the idea of a military panel survey is exciting, as of now it appears to be a solution in search of a compelling problem. Given the relatively unexplored power of matching discussed in earlier chapters, the incremental need for a military panel data set appears yet to be established.

Arguments Against a Military Panel Data Set

Two arguments against a military panel survey are clear: cost and the incremental contribution of surveys given the existing availability of administrative data.

Cost

Budgets are all too finite, and such a panel survey is likely to be very expensive. Panel surveys must adopt survey methods that ensure high response rates (90-plus percent per survey); otherwise, they are not truly panel data sets. Such panel methods are likely to be expensive, perhaps $250 per case.

How large would a panel survey need to be to be useful? Note that many policy issues would focus on a subset of the population or suggest comparisons across subgroups—for example, junior service persons rather than senior service persons, comparing responses across racial and ethnic groups, exploring the experiences of veterans (assuming that people were being followed even after they left the military). This brief discussion suggests a sample of several thousand individuals. Simple multiplication therefore suggests an annual budget of well over $1 million. There would also be start-up costs of similar magnitude. Even then, the resulting military panel survey would be too small to support many subgroup analyses.

Incremental Contribution

Civilian labor market analysts developed longitudinal panel surveys to collect information over time on key labor market outcomes: employment, occupation, earnings, location, and family structure. As we noted earlier, for individuals in the military, as the employer, DoD already has access to the administrative data with that information. Compared to survey data, the administrative data provide larger samples, higher quality, and lower cost. Furthermore, as discussed in previous chapters, such administrative data can be augmented as needed by linking to military (or civilian) survey data. Thus, the first challenge for proponents of a military panel survey will be defining the need.

Two Justifications for a Military Panel Survey

Clearly, the justification for a military panel survey will involve the need for information not available in administrative data. That military manpower policy analysis has a need for information not contained in the administrative data is the justification for the ongoing DMDC cross-sectional survey effort (e.g., the SOFS program).

One approach to justifying a military panel survey is therefore to explore the need for *longitudinal* information on the items already collected in DMDC's cross-sectional surveys: retention intentions, readiness, global stress levels, and overall satisfaction. We can thus recast our question: How useful would longitudinal data on these outcomes be?

To begin, note that many analyses with these measures do not require longitudinal data. Thus, we could explore the relation between retention intentions (or spousal attitudes or marital satisfaction) and actual retention by matching a cross-sectional survey with subsequent administrative data on retention (see the discussion of Hosek, Kavanaugh, and Miller, 2006, in Chapter Four). Similarly, we could explore the relation of deployment to spousal attitudes using administrative data on deployment matched to subsequent cross-sectional survey data (again, Hosek has such analyses under way).

The Need for Truly Longitudinal Information

However, some analysis strategies do require longitudinal military data. For example, if we want to relate one outcome measured only in surveys to another, later, outcome also measured only in surveys, then we would need longitudinal military survey data. As an enumerative exercise, generating such combinations is easy: Pick any two outcomes measured in the survey (e.g., what is the relation between spousal attitudes towards military service last year and marital satisfaction today?). However, we have been unable to identify any such combination that has a compelling enough role in military manpower analysis to justify the large cost of a military panel survey.

Controls for Confounders

An additional advantage of panel data appears to generate a stronger case for a longitudinal survey. In cross-sectional analyses, it is difficult to determine to what extent observed relations are causal versus simply the result of selection. Thus, for example, if we would observe that marital satisfaction is lower among those with frequent deployments, at least two explanations are possible. One is *causal*: Frequent deployment causes a decrease in marital satisfaction. The other is *selection*: Those who deploy more often would have had lower marital satisfaction even in the absence of deployment.

One way to distinguish between these two explanations is to use longitudinal data. Specifically, an analyst would explore the change in marital satisfaction with deployment.[1] Implementing this approach requires longitudinal data; in other words, we need measurements on marital satisfaction—for the same person—at two points in time (before and after the deployment). See Appendix A for a formal development of this idea (see also Angrist and Krueger, 2001).

However, this argument for panel data is incomplete. Often such control for confounders can be accomplished with repeated cross-sectional data (e.g., the SOFS effort) and appropriate methods. As Heckman and Robb (1985, p. 159) argue,

> Longitudinal data are widely regarded as a panacea for selection and simultaneity problems. . . . Our conclusions are startling. Provided that conventional fixed effects specifications of earnings functions are adopted, there is no need to use longitudinal data to identify the impact of training on earnings. Estimators based on repeated cross-section data for unrelated persons identify the same parameter. . . . A major conclusion of our chapter is that the relative benefits of longitudinal data have been overstated, because the potential benefits of cross-section and repeated cross-section data have been understated.

To understand these ideas in the military manpower context, consider trying to model the effect of deployment on marital satisfaction (or intentions to reenlist). The natural approach is to examine the change in marital satisfaction for a given person from before to after deployment, ideally, using a control group that did not deploy (i.e., a difference-of-difference design).

Note, however, that this design does not really require individual panel data. We could instead take two waves of the Status of Forces survey, and use administrative data to divide the population in each wave into those who would and those who would not deploy between the two waves. Then, we could estimate the difference in average marital satisfaction among those who (would) deploy across the two surveys. The two samples are both random samples from the same population. The difference in outcomes is therefore a proper estimate of the difference in outcomes for the group as a whole.

There are some technical issues. First, the two estimates have sampling variability. For discussion of appropriate methods for such analyses of repeated cross-sectional data, see Deaton (1985) and Veerbek and Nijman (1993). Second, this approach will often require relatively large cross-sectional samples (to allow precise estimates of the group means). Note, however, that the SOFS samples are already quite large. Conversely, the equivalent approach on true panel data will require total samples large enough to include subsamples of those who get the "treatment" (e.g., deployment) in a given period. Conventional panel surveys are often too small to allow such analyses. Third, note that repeated cross-sectional surveys are not subject to the concerns about high response rates (with their corresponding much higher per-case costs) and the concerns about differential sample attrition when (as is inevitably true) sample attrition is large and sometimes differential (Hausman and Wise, 1979; Fitzgerald, Gottschalk, and Moffitt, 1998; Lillard and Panis, 1998).

---

[1] Ideally, that change would be compared to the change in marital satisfaction among otherwise similar individuals who were not deployed.

Finally, note also that this approach extends the earlier discussion of matching cross-sectional military survey data to military administrative data. The ability to match later outcomes measured in administrative data makes repeated cross-sectional data *more* powerful in the military context than in the civilian context. Specifically, we can use the link to the administrative data to ex post identify the people that will later get the "treatment" (e.g., deployment).

Some Design Issues

This, then, is the challenge for those advocating the initiation of a new longitudinal military panel survey effort: What are the policy issues that either require true panel data or benefit from the analysis of changes to eliminate confounders? And are those policy issues sufficiently important and sufficiently poorly measured in administrative data to justify the considerable expenditure required to run a panel survey? The previous paragraphs provide two approaches to making such an argument.

The details of that justification will then be crucial for the design of such a military panel survey effort. The simplest design for a military panel survey would be to select a random sample of new entrants (active duty and non–prior service [NPS] reservists) every year and follow them forward. The survey could be initialized with a corresponding sample of earlier entrants. For that sample of earlier entrants, one could collect some information using retrospective survey questions. Some other information would be filled in using administrative data (e.g., MEPCOM files and WEX). Other information (e.g., earlier attitudes) is probably not recoverable.

This "simple design" raises several issues: sample frame, following (or tracking) rules, sample refreshing, and sample size.

Sample Frame

Is the sample to be selected only from new recruits to the active forces or also from new NPS reservists? Are cross-service comparisons a crucial area of interest? If so, we would probably want to select approximately equal-sized samples from each service. Otherwise, the smaller services will have smaller samples making tests of differences across services inconclusive.

Following Rules

Are sampled individuals going to be followed (i.e., continue to be surveyed) after they leave the military? Presumably, if the sample includes reservists, then active-duty people would be followed into the reserves. However, some people enter the reserves only with a gap. Often, people leave the reserves and then return. These two career paths suggest following ex-service people for several years, even if they have not yet entered the reserves. Perhaps they will subsequently enter the reserves. Interest in the transition to civilian life itself provides another reason to follow veterans for at least a year or two. Longer follow-up periods would probably be appropriate as part of a joint effort with the Department of Veterans Affairs (DVA). DVA is currently considering an expanded survey effort.

Sample Refreshing

The military is nearly a closed personnel system. There is only minimal lateral entry. It follows that the sample at later grades or years of service will be much smaller than the sample at lower grades or years of service. This may be acceptable. Alternatively, the sample could be refreshed by drawing in additional people at more senior ranks. The natural point to refresh the sample is as service persons enter the "career force" and the probability of exit drops sharply (i.e., somewhere between 8 and 12 years of service). Of course, as with over-sampling in the NLS-Y, there would be no earlier history for those people. Thus, some of the advantage of a longitudinal design would be lost.[2]

Sample Size

Hanging over any design of a military panel survey is the issue of sample size. A military panel survey would have two cost components. There are some fixed costs, independent of survey size. These include design, instrument development, much of data cleaning, and dissemination. Most of the costs are variable, almost directly proportional to sample size and probably well over $250 per interview

From an analytic perspective, larger samples are preferred to smaller samples. The NLS-Y samples have included more than 10,000 participants. Other major panel surveys are also in that range. The PSID today surveys about 8,000 families (Panel Study of Income Dynamics, undated). The first follow-up to the National Education Longitudinal Survey interviewed nearly 20,000 people (Modi, 2000). The SIPP varied in size, but was often much larger.

However, the larger the sample, the more expensive the effort. The natural approach to this trade-off is to use classical power analyses for the leading substantive justifications for the longitudinal military survey effort. Those power calculations are likely to be sensitive to the extent to which analyses refer to the entire survey sample (versus only to a subsample) and the extent to which cross-subgroup comparisons are required. Thus, a panel to explore issues for more senior enlisted individuals or for only officers or one to compare outcomes for the Army to outcomes for the Air Force would need to be much larger than a survey intended to explore outcomes for the entire survey sample.

Note also that, if the justification for the longitudinal panel is better control for confounders, the required sample sizes are likely to be even larger. Only individuals who have experienced a change between two surveys will contribute to the analysis. Thus, for the example of the effect of deployment on marital satisfaction, the power calculations will be driven by the number of people who are deployed between the two interviews. That number is likely to be much smaller than the entire survey sample.

Some Military Panel Surveys

At the beginning of this chapter, we noted that there is no "military panel survey." That statement is only partially true. In this section, we briefly discuss two exceptions: The Minnesota National Guard Panel and the Millennium Cohort Study.

---

[2] See the earlier discussion about additional retrospective survey questions for older survey members at the establishment of a panel survey. The loss in quality from such retrospective questions could be gauged directly by also asking such retrospective questions of the panel sample. Those retrospective responses could then be compared to their prospective responses.

Minnesota National Guard Panel

In support of the Global War on Terrorism, the 1st Brigade Combat Team of the Minnesota National Guard was deployed for the longest combat tour of any unit—Regular Army, National Guard, or U.S. Army Reserve—22 months activation, 16 months in Iraq (Minnesota National Guard, 2007; Nohrenberg, 2007). Partially in response to concern about the effects of such a long period of activation and deployment, the Minnesota National Guard has established a special pilot reunion-and-reintegration program (Roos and Sanford, 2007).

To track the reintegration experiences of this population and to understand the services they received, DMDC has fielded a panel survey effort. Specifically, the December 2007 SOFS-R sample was augmented with 3,209 Minnesota National Guard members to whom the pilot reunion and reintegration program was offered. DMDC plans to include these same individuals in future SOFS-Rs (e.g., June and November 2008).

The Millennium Cohort Study

Begun in 2001, the Millennium Cohort Study aims to enroll 140,000 military personnel and to interview them every three years during a 21-year period. Following a design suggested by a National Academy of Sciences study (Hernandez et al., 1999), interviews are to occur through a combination of mail-out/mail-back and the Internet. To address concerns about response rates and nonresponse bias, there is to be limited telephone follow-up of nonrespondents. For more on the Study, see Gray et al. (2002) and the study Web site (U.S. Department of Defense, undated).

Modeled on the 1976 Nurses Cohort Study and the 1948 Framingham Heart Study, the study is explicitly a reaction to concerns about "Gulf War Illness" and related long-term effects of deployment and combat. Consistent with this motivation, the interview and the associated matching to administrative records are focused on health issues. The interest in long-term effects on health motivates the panel structure and following military personnel well after they leave the military.

Despite this health focus, the data collection effort appears to have considerable potential for the analysis of military manpower issues. The samples are large. Some demographic data are collected. The health data should be of use for many military manpower issues. The projected linkage to military administrative data is robust and of great potential utility to military manpower research (see the discussion in Chapter Six). For military manpower studies, interviews more frequently than every three years might have been preferable, but doing so would have increased costs and burden (probably leading to lower response rates). Obviously, continuing to add additional cohorts will increase the utility of the effort.

CHAPTER TEN

Discussion

This report has reviewed possible data strategies in support of military manpower policy analysis, surveying the existing rich administrative and survey data resources provided and supported by DMDC, pointing out the power of existing data matches to SSA earnings data, and noting the potential of matches to other data (e.g., to DMDC survey data, to the ACS). For researchers (and those sponsoring research), the primary insight of this report is that there appear to be several underexploited data analysis strategies that involve matching DoD administrative data to DoD survey data, non-DoD administrative data, and non-DoD survey data. Precedents for each of these approaches exist, but actual analyses are rare and often just now appearing. These approaches are likely to face significant (and appropriate) human subjects issues, but it should be possible to address those issues.

Overall, DoD has a robust data development and dissemination system. However, it is certainly not perfect, and data managers and those who fund data collection efforts should continue their efforts to improve it. Streamlining procedures for data matching is likely to be much less expensive than engaging in major new data collection efforts (e.g., participation in civilian panel surveys, an expanded military cross-sectional survey effort, a new military panel survey effort). Until the benefit of these new matching approaches is better understood, DoD is urged to proceed with caution on any major new data collection effort.

Spread throughout this paper are specific recommendations—some related to this broad guidance, some unrelated. We summarize them below in three groups: minimal cost, moderate cost, and major cost. The recommendations are numbered, with the numeral preceding the decimal indicating the chapter in which the recommendation is first made, and the numeral after the decimal indicating the order in which the recommendations appear within the chapter.

DMDC supports specific analyses and studies for OUSD/P&R. DMDC alone might study these recommendations, but DMDC would only implement them with the approval of OUSD/P&R. OUSD/P&R would approve them only with clear evidence of their utility in support of studies and analyses. Thus, while the recommendations below are addressed to DMDC, their implementation would require agreement at higher levels. We hope that this document and this list of recommendations will spur the research community to consider using some of the data strategies described here.

Minimal Cost

Recommendation 2.1: DMDC should consider mechanisms for more widely disseminating the knowledge of its file managers to the non-DMDC analysts and programmers who work with those data. Web logs (i.e., blogs or wikis) seem like attractive possibilities. Such efforts often get caught up in the need to vet each posting. Some mechanism to lower the implied quality required, and thus the burden of posting such issues, would also be useful.

Recommendation 2.2: DMDC should review its current archiving practices and best practices in comparable institutions. Is all the data collected properly archived? Are there other key data that should be captured? For example, analyses of enlistment and reenlistment would benefit from data on which occupational specialties offer enlistment and reenlistment bonuses and the bonus amount (or "step"). However, that information is not currently captured.[1]

Recommendation 5.1: DMDC should explore whether likely use of matched SSA earnings data and DMDC administrative data is sufficiently intensive to justify regularizing the current ad hoc matching arrangements (including the required steps under the Privacy Act).

Moderate Cost

Recommendation 3.1: DMDC should consider exploring the effect of nonresponse bias on its survey efforts. Some form of double sampling appears to be a promising strategy—that is, selecting a subsample of the universe for intensive follow-up (e.g., attempting phone contact). We note, however, that the emerging academic consensus is that low response rates are less of an issue than had been previously thought.

Recommendation 4.1: DMDC should explore alternative approaches to matching DMDC survey data to DMDC administrative data that would allow easier and more detailed analyses while preserving the confidentiality of survey respondents. A cold room approach seems worthy of further consideration.

Recommendation 6.1: DMDC should explore whether likely use of DMDC administrative data matched to ACS data (e.g., for information on employment and education of reservists and veterans) is sufficiently promising to justify conducting a one-time match. Depending on the utility of that one-time match, DMDC might consider regularizing matches with ACS data.

Major Cost

Recommendation 7.1: DoD should explore low-level participation in any proposed NLS-Y2010, but higher-level participation does not seem warranted. The proposed structure of that survey suggests that it will be of only limited use in military manpower research. Furthermore,

---

[1] Such concerns about incomplete contextual data arise in other domains (e.g., welfare policy and food and nutrition policy).

it does not appear that any simple addition to that effort would be of clear and dramatic value to DoD.

Recommendation 8.1: DoD should explore augmenting the existing SOFS-R effort with a more intensive survey (of a much smaller sample). Such a survey would probably include a longer interview, with psychometric measures for mental health and relational quality. Such an exploration should consider the possible uses of such an intensive survey and the importance of those uses for DoD manpower policy analysis.

Recommendation 9.1: DoD should explore the potential uses of a military panel survey. As a start to such exploration, DoD should consider its experience with the collection and use of its panel survey of selected members of the Minnesota National Guard (as discussed in Chapter Nine). In addition, any such exploration should consider the place of such a military panel survey in the context of both the rich, available, longitudinal administrative data and the possibility of linking that administrative data to the existing cross-sectional survey data (or to richer cross-sectional survey data; see Recommendation 4.1).

APPENDIX A

Formal Discussion of Some Technical Issues

Consistent with its projected dual audience, the body of this document presents a nontechnical discussion of the issues. To complement that nontechnical discussion, this appendix presents a brief and more formal discussion of several of the issues raised in the body of the report.

Nonresponse Bias

We argued in the body of the text that low response rates are potentially problematic. We informally argued that the larger the nonresponse rate, the larger the potential bias. Here, we present a simple formal model that supports that argument. See Horvitz and Thomson (1952) for an early discussion of this issue. See Groves (1989) for a more modern discussion.

Suppose we are interested in estimating the mean, μ, from a population. A fraction, ρ, of the population will not respond. What is the bias, B, in our estimate of the mean from the population that does respond?

$$B = \mu_R - \mu = \mu_R - \{(1-\rho)\mu_R + \rho\mu_M\} = \rho(\mu_R - \mu_N)$$

For the above equation, μ is the true mean, μ_R is the mean among respondents, and μ_N is the mean among nonrespondents. The larger the fraction of nonrespondents, ρ, and the larger the difference between the mean response of the respondents and the nonrespondents, the larger the bias will be. If the respondents and nonrespondents do not differ on the response of interest, then the nonresponse induces no bias.

Furthermore, when the outcome is bounded (e.g., a binary outcome, or an outcome with a plausible bound on the mean), the range of the possible bias due to nonresponse is linear in the size of the nonresponse. Thus, more-intense field methods (i.e., those that include everyone who would have been included by the original method plus some more people) always shrink the possible range. However, it is possible that doing so will not shrink the actual bias. This perverse case will occur when the subpopulation added has a mean on the "other" side of the mean of those found using the less-intense method from those not found under either method. In most cases, this scenario is implausible. We usually expect those found using more-intense methods to be between those found using less-intense methods and those not found using either method.

Choice-Based Sampling

CBS has most commonly been applied in the case of military recruiting. Note that there are two populations: those who enlist and those who do not enlist. Civilian surveys have many people in the second group, but few people in the first group. Military surveys (or administrative data) have people only in the first group. We know the size of the entire (youth) population, N. We know the number of people who enlist, N_E, so we can compute the number of people who do not enlist (N_C) by subtraction: $N_C = N - N_E$. Finally, to simplify the notation below, denote by ρ the fraction of enlistees in the population:

$$\rho = \frac{N_E}{N_C + N_E}$$

Consider the case in which we have two random samples. First, we have a random sample of size M_G from the general population (including enlistees). Second, we have another random sample of size M_E from the enlisted population only. In this case, we can view the resulting population as a random sample from the nonenlisting population and a random sample from the enlisting population. Since we know the size of the two populations, we can therefore treat the combined population as a stratified random sample, in which the weights for the two groups can be constructed from the size of the two populations and the size of the two samples. For our specific example, the weights would be

$$w_C = \frac{N_C}{(1-\rho)M_G} \qquad w_E = \frac{N_E}{\rho M_G + M_E}$$

Analysis can then proceed using weighted methods (e.g., the computation of means, medians, and percentiles, as well as regressions, logistic regressions, and most more-complicated analytic methods).

The insight and the general approach are not limited to the specific two-group-and-two-random-sample case considered here. The basic insight generalizes to larger numbers of groups, to the case where the samples are nonoverlapping, to the case where the population fractions are themselves estimates, and to other cases. Furthermore, depending on the exact data configuration, other methodological approaches beyond weighted analyses may be available and will sometimes be more efficient. See, for example, Amemiya (1985, §9.5). See Pudney (1989, §2.5.2) for a related discussion.

Fixed-Effects Analysis

The body of this report argued that panel data are useful for making causal inferences from observational data. Formally, our argument proceeds as follows. Consider a regression of the form

$$y_{i,t} = \alpha + X_{i,t}\beta + Z_{i,t}\gamma + \varepsilon_{i,t}; \quad \varepsilon_{i,t} = \mu_i + \eta_{i,t}$$

We seek to estimate the causal effect of X on y; i.e., holding everything else fixed, how much would y change if we changed X? Continuing the example in the body of the report, y might be marital satisfaction and X might be deployment. That is, consider the same individual, comparing his marital satisfaction if he were deployed in some period to his marital satisfaction if he were not deployed in the same period.

Clearly, we cannot both deploy and not deploy an individual. Some other statistical technique must be used. Regression will estimate the causal effect if the unobservables, ε, are not related to the key independent variable, X (after we control for Z). So for example, if people with low marital satisfaction volunteer to be deployed, then this condition is violated. We do not observe the low marital satisfaction, so it is captured in the unobservables, ε. If this scenario dominates, then deployment will appear to decrease marital satisfaction, even if there is no true causal effect.

One approach is to include more proxies in Z. The more proxies in Z, the fewer things that might induce a relation between the unobservables and deployment. However, it is hard to imagine what proxies might be useful in a cross-sectional survey. Conventional wisdom is that such proxies are rarely sufficient.

Another approach to this problem is to note that we might rephrase the research question as "Does deployment lower marital satisfaction?" That is, for a given individual, will deployment cause marital satisfaction to decline from before deployment to after deployment? The questions are not identical. At the very least, we would want to "control" for normal changes in marital satisfaction. But the heuristic is useful.

Following the logic of this heuristic, we might relate the change in X (ΔX) to the change in y (Δy):

$$\Delta y_{i,t} = \Delta X_{i,t}\beta + \Delta Z_{i,t}\gamma + \Delta\varepsilon_{i,t};\quad \Delta\varepsilon_{i,t} = \Delta\eta_{i,t}$$

Such "differencing" will eliminate any relation between marital satisfaction and deployment caused by (approximately) time-invariant factors—i.e., is it a "good" marriage. In the equation, such time-invariant factors are represented by μ_i.

This analysis is correct but incomplete. There is a large body of literature on when such differencing approaches will work and generalizations to this approach. The interested reader is referred to Stock and Watson (2003) for a clear, nontechnical discussion.

APPENDIX B

U.S. Census Bureau Residence Rules

This appendix provides the verbatim 2000 Census language about the treatment of "usual residence" (and "Residence Rules," more broadly). The text is copied from U.S. Census Bureau (2003).

Military or Merchant Marine Personnel in the United States

People in the military residing in the United States: Counted at their usual residence (the place where they live and sleep most of the time), whether it is on-base or off-base.

Crews of military vessels with a U.S. homeport: Counted at their usual onshore residence if they report one (the place where they live and sleep most of the time when they are onshore) or otherwise at their vessel's homeport.

Crews of U.S. flag merchant vessels engaged in inland waterway transportation: Counted at their usual onshore residence (the place where they live and sleep most of the time when they are onshore).

Crews of U.S. flag merchant vessels docked in a U.S. port or sailing from one U.S. port to another U.S. port: Counted at their usual onshore residence if they report one (the place where they live and sleep most of the time when they are onshore) or otherwise on the vessel.

Military or Merchant Marine Personnel Outside the United States

People in the military assigned to military installations outside the U.S., including family members with them: Counted as part of the U.S. overseas population and not as part of the U.S. resident population.

Crews of military vessels with a homeport outside the U.S.: Counted as part of the U.S. overseas population and not as part of the U.S. resident population.

Crews of U.S. flag merchant vessels docked in a foreign port, sailing from one foreign port to another foreign port, sailing from a U.S. port to a foreign port, or sailing from a foreign port to a U.S. port: Not included in the census.

APPENDIX C

Survey Veteran Questions

This appendix provides the exact wording of questions about veteran status for three large U.S. Census Bureau surveys—the Current Population Survey, the 2000 Decennial Census, and the American Community Survey. Actual questions are in bold. Official Census Bureau clarification is in regular text. Responses are indented.

Current Population Survey

Did you ever serve on active duty in the U.S. Armed Forces?

When did you serve?

1 Vietnam Era (8/64–4/75)

2 Korean War (6/50–1/55)

3 World War II (9/40–7/47)

4 World War I (4/17–11/18)

5 Other Service (All Other Periods)

6 Nonveteran

Are you now in the Armed Forces?

2000 Decennial Census

20.a. Has this person ever served on active duty in the U.S. Armed Forces, military Reserves, or National Guard? Active duty does not include training for the Reserves or National Guard, but DOES include activation, for example, for the Persian Gulf War.

Yes, now on active duty

Yes, on active duty in past, but not now

No, training for Reserves or National Guard

Guard only -> Skip to 21

No, never served in the military -> Skip to 21

20.b. When did this person serve on active duty in the U.S. Armed Forces? Mark a box for EACH period in which this person served.

April 1995 or later

Some other time

World War II (September 1940–July 1947)

Korean conflict (June 1950–January 1955)

February 1955 to July 1964

Vietnam era (August 1964–April 1975)

May 1975 to August 1980

September 1980 to July 1990

August 1990 to March 1995 (including Persian Gulf War)

20.c. In total, how many years of active-duty military service has this person had?

Less than 2 years

2 years or more

American Community Survey

20. Has this person ever served on active duty in the U.S. Armed Forces, military Reserves, or National Guard? Active duty does not include training for the Reserves or National Guard, but DOES include activation, for example, for the Persian Gulf War.

Yes, now on active duty

Yes, on active duty during the last 12 months, but not now

Yes, on active duty in the past, but not during the last 12 months

No, training for Reserves or National Guard only -> Skip to question 23

No, never served in the military -> Skip to question 23

21. When did this person serve on active duty in the U.S. Armed Forces? Mark (X) a box for EACH period in which this person served, even if just for part of the period.

September 2001 or later

August 1990 to August 2001 (including Persian Gulf War)

September 1980 to July 1990

May 1975 to August 1980

Vietnam era (August 1964 to April 1975)

March 1961 to July 1964

Korean War (July 1950 to January 1955)

World War II (December 1941 to December 1946)

22. In total, how many years of active-duty military service has this person had?

Less than 2 years

2 years or more

References

Amemiya, Takeshi, *Advanced Econometrics,* Cambridge, Mass.: Harvard University Press, 1985.

Angrist, Joshua D., "Lifetime Earnings and the Vietnam Era Draft Lottery: Evidence from Social Security Administrative Records," *The American Economic Review,* Vol. 80, No. 3, June 1990, pp. 313–336.

———, "Estimating the Labor Market Impact of Voluntary Military Service Using Social Security Data on Military Applicants," *Econometrica,* Vol. 66, No. 2, March 1998, pp. 249–289.

Angrist, Joshua D., and Alan B. Krueger, "Why Do World War II Veterans Earn More Than Nonveterans?" *Journal of Labor Economics,* Vol. 12, No. 1, January 1994, pp. 74–97.

———, "Empirical Strategies in Labor Economics," in Orley Ashenfelter and David Cards, eds., *Handbook of Labor Economics Vol. 3a,* Amsterdam, N.Y.: North-Holland, 2001.

Antel, John J., James Hosek, and Christine E. Peterson, *Military Enlistment and Attrition: An Analysis of Decision Reversal,* Santa Monica, Calif.: RAND Corporation, R-3510-FMP, 1987. As of July 26, 2007: http://www.rand.org/pubs/reports/R3510/

Asch, Beth J., M. Rebecca Kilburn, and Jacob Alex Klerman, *Attracting College-Bound Youth into the Military: Toward the Development of New Recruiting Policy Options,* Santa Monica, Calif.: RAND Corporation, MR-984-OSD, 1999. As of July 26, 2007:
http://www.rand.org/pubs/monograph_reports/MR984/

Biemer, Paul P., Robert M. Groves, Lars E. Lyberg, Nancy A. Mathiowetz, and Seymour Sudman, ed., *Measurement Error in Surveys,* New York: Wiley, 1991.

Black, Dan, and Julia Lane, "Report on Task 1: The Labor Market Trajectories of 20–24 Year Old Veterans," National Opinion Research Center, University of Chicago, January 1, 2007. As of July 26, 2007: http://www.dol.gov/vets/research/trajectories_rev.pdf

Brady, H. E., and S. Luks, "Defining Welfare Spells: Coping with Problems of Survey Responses and Administrative Data," paper presented at the American Political Science Association meeting, Chicago, Ill., August 30, 1995.

Bregger, John E., "The Current Population Survey: A Historical Perspective and the BLS' Role," *Monthly Labor Review Online,* Vol. 107, No. 6, June 1984, pp. 8–14. As of July 26, 2007:
http://www.bls.gov/opub/mlr/1984/06/art2full.pdf

Caplan, J. R., "Understanding Nonresponse in Employee Populations: Who, What, and Why?" PowerPoint briefing presented at the 13th Annual Forecasters Conference, Washington, D.C., September 18, 2003.

Data Sharing for Demographic Research, "Data Sharing for Demographic Research: Disseminating Data," undated Web page. As of July 27, 2007:
http://www.icpsr.umich.edu/DSDR/deposit.html

Deaton, Angus, "Panel Data from Time Series of Cross-Sections," *Journal of Econometrics,* Vol. 30, Nos. 1–2, October –November 1985, pp. 109–126.

Defense Manpower Data Center, *May 2004 Status of Forces Survey of Reserve Component Members: Administration, Datasets, and Codebook,* DMDC Report No. 2004-013, Arlington, Va., 2004.

———, *DMDC Profile: Information and Technology for Better Decision Making*, Arlington, Va., 2006. As of August 8, 2007, available to authorized personnel at:
http://smspsint.rand.org/sites/FRP_SSA_Project/default.aspx

———, *November 2006 Status of Forces Survey of DoD Civilian Employees: Leading Indicators*, Arlington, Va., March 29, 2007a.

———, *December 2006 Status of Forces Survey of Reserve Component Members: Leading Indicators*, Arlington, Va., April 4, 2007b.

———, *December 2006 Status of Forces Survey of Active-Duty Members: Leading Indicators*, Arlington, Va., April 6, 2007c.

———, daily responses to the *May 2007 Status of Forces Survey of Active-Duty Members* (unpublished raw data), 2007d.

———, "July 2002 Status of Forces Survey of Active-Duty Members: Web vs. Web and Paper Results," PowerPoint briefing presented at the meeting of the Inter-Service Survey Coordinating Committee, Monterey, Calif., May 14–15, 2007e.

DMDC—*see* Defense Manpower Data Center.

Fitzgerald, John, Peter Gottschalk, and Robert Moffitt, "An Analysis of Sample Attrition in Panel Data: The Michigan Panel Study of Income Dynamics," *Journal of Human Resources*, Vol. 33, No. 2, Spring 1998, pp. 251–299.

Goldberg, Matthew S., and John T. Warner, "Military Experience, Civilian Experience, and the Earnings of Veterans," *Journal of Human Resources*, Vol. 22, No. 1, Winter 1987, pp. 62–81.

Gray, Gregory C., Chesbrough, K.B., Ryan, M.A., Amoroso, P., Boyko, E.J., Gackstetter, G.D., Hooper, T.I., and Riddle, J.R., "The Millennium Cohort Study: A 21-Year Prospective Cohort Study of 140,000 Military Personnel," *Military Medicine*, Vol. 167, No. 6, June 2002, p. 483–486.

Groves, Robert M., *Survey Errors and Survey Costs*, New York: John Wiley and Sons, Inc., 1989.

———, "Nonresponse Rates and Nonresponse Bias in Household Surveys," *Public Opinion Quarterly*, Vol. 70, No. 5, special issue, 2006, pp. 646–675.

Groves, Robert M., Grant Benson, William D. Mosher, Jennifer Rosenbaum, Peter Granda, William Axinn, James Lepkowski, and Anjani Chandra., "Plan and Operation of Cycle 6 of the National Survey of Family Growth: Data from the Program and Collection Procedures," *Vital Health Statistics*, Series 1, No. 45, August 2005. As of August 22, 2007:
http://www.cdc.gov/nchs/data/series/sr_01/sr01_042.pdf

Groves, Robert M., and Steven G. Heeringa, "Responsive Design for Household Surveys: Tools for Actively Controlling Survey Errors and Costs," *Journal of the Royal Statistical Society: Series A*, Vol. 169, No. 3, July 2006, pp. 439–457.

Harrell, Margaret C., Nelson Lim, Laura Werber Castaneda, and Daniela Golinelli, *Working Around the Military: Challenges to Military Spouse Employment and Education*, Santa Monica, Calif.: RAND Corporation, MG-196-OSD, 2004. As of July 26, 2007:
http://www.rand.org/pubs/monographs/MG196/

Hausman, Jerry A., and David A. Wise, "Attrition Bias in Experimental and Panel Data: The Gary Income Maintenance Experiment," *Econometrica*, Vol. 47, No. 2, March 1979, pp. 455–474.

Heckman, James J., and Richard Robb, "Alternative Methods for Evaluating the Impact of Interventions," in James J. Heckman and Burton Singer, eds., *Longitudinal Analysis of Labor Market Data*, Cambridge, UK: Cambridge University Press, 1985.

Hernandez, Lyla M., Durch, Jane S., Blazer, Dan G. II, and Hoverman, Isabel V., eds., *Gulf War Veterans: Measuring Health*, Washington, D.C.: National Academy Press, 1999.

Hill, C., V. Joseph Hotz, Charles H. Mullin, and John Karl Scholz, *EITC Eligibility, Participation and Compliance Rates for AFDC Households: Evidence from the California Caseload*, unpublished manuscript, University of Chicago, Chicago, Ill., May 1997.

Horvitz, D. G., and D. J. Thompson, "A Generalization of Sampling Without Replacement from a Finite Universe," *Journal of the American Statistical Association*, Vol. 47, No. 260, December 1952, pp. 663 685.

Hosek, James, *An Introduction to Estimation with Choice-Based Sample Data*, Santa Monica, Calif.: RAND Corporation, P-6361, 1979.

Hosek, James, and Christine E. Peterson, *The AFEES-NLS Database: A Choice-Based Sample for Studying Enlistment and Post-Enlistment Outcomes*, Santa Monica, Calif.: RAND Corporation, N-1930-MRAL, 1983. As of July 26, 2007:
http://www.rand.org/pubs/notes/N1930/

———, *Reenlistment Bonuses and Retention Behavior*, Santa Monica, Calif.: RAND Corporation, R-3199-MIL, 1985. As of July 26, 2007:
http://www.rand.org/pubs/reports/R3199/

———, *Serving Her Country: An Analysis of Women's Enlistments*, Santa Monica, Calif.: RAND Corporation, R-3853-FMP, 1990.

Hosek, James, Jennifer Kavanaugh, and Laura Miller, *How Deployments Affects Service Members*, Santa Monica, Calif.: RAND Corporation, MG-432-RC, 2006. As of August 22, 2007:
http://www.rand.org/pubs/monographs/MG432/

Hosek, James, Beth J. Asch, C. Christine Fair, Craig Martin, and Michael Mattock, *Married to the Military: The Employment and Earnings of Military Wives Compared with Those of Civilian Wives*, Santa Monica, Calif.: RAND Corporation, MR-1565-OSD, 2002. As of July 26, 2007:
http://www.rand.org/pubs/monograph_reports/MR1565/

Hotz, V. Joseph, Robert Goerge, Julie Balzekas, and Francis Margolin, eds., "Administrative Data for Policy-Relevant Research: Assessment of Current Utility and Recommendations for Development," report of the Advisory Panel on Research Uses of Administrative Data of the Northwestern University/University of Chicago Joint Center for Poverty Research, January 1998. As of July 26, 2007:
http://www.jcpr.org/wpfiles/AdminData_FullReport.pdf

Karney, Benjamin R., and John S. Crown, *Families Under Stress: An Assessment of Data, Theory, and Research on Marriage and Divorce in the Military*, Santa Monica, Calif.: RAND Corporation, MG-599-OSD, 2007. As of August 22, 2007:
http://www.rand.org/pubs/monographs/MG599/

Keeter, Scott, Carolyn Miller, Andrew Kohut, Robert M. Groves, and Stanley Presser, "Consequences of Reducing Nonresponse in a National Telephone Survey," *Public Opinion Quarterly*, Vol. 64, No. 2, Summer 2000, pp. 125–148.

Kessler, Ronald C., J. A. Little, and Robert M. Groves, "Advances in Strategies for Minimizing and Adjusting for Survey Nonresponse," *Epidemiologic Reviews*, Vol. 17, No. 1, 1995, pp. 192–204.

Lillard, Lee A., and Constantijn W. A. Panis, "Panel Attrition from the Panel Study of Income Dynamics: Household Income, Marital Status, and Mortality," *Journal of Human Resources*, Vol. 33, No. 2, Spring 1998, pp. 437–457.

Lim, Nelson, Daniela Golinelli, and Michelle Cho, *"Working Around the Military" Revisited: Spouse Employment in the 2000 Census Data*, Santa Monica, Calif.: RAND Corporation, MG-566-OSD, 2007. As of July 26, 2007:
http://www.rand.org/pubs/monographs/MG566/

Loughran, David S., Jacob Alex Klerman, and Craig Martin, *Activation and the Earnings of Reservists*, Santa Monica, Calif.: RAND Corporation, MG-474-OSD, 2006. As of July 26, 2007:
http://www.rand.org/pubs/monographs/MG474/

Martorell, Francisco, Jacob Alex Klerman, and David S. Loughran, *How Do Earnings Change When reservists Are Activated?: A Reconciliation of Estimates Derived from Survey and Administrative Data*, Santa Monica, Calif.: RAND Corporation, TR-565-OSD, 2008.

Minnesota National Guard, *2007 Annual Report*, 2007.

Modi, Manisha, "National Education Longitudinal Survey," *Surveys Measuring Well-Being*, September 14, 2000. As of July 27, 2007:
http://nber.org/~kling/surveys/NELS88.htm

Nohrenberg, Amber, "National Guard Troops Happy to Be Home," Minnesota National Guard Web site, July 18, 2007. As of May 16, 2008:
http://www.minnesotanationalguard.org/press_room/e-zine/articles/index.php?item=883

OMB—*see* U.S. Office of Budget Management.

Orvis, Bruce R., *Validity and Usefulness of Enlistment Intention Information*, Santa Monica, Calif.: RAND Corporation, R-3775-FMP, 1992.

Panel Study of Income Dynamics, home page, undated. As of July 27, 2007:
http://psidonline.isr.umich.edu/

Pierret, Charles, "Preliminary Strategies for Fielding the NLSY2010," Bureau of Labor Statistics memo, 2006.

Prevost, Ron, "Health Related Administrative Records Research," presentation at the Department of Health and Human Services National Committee on Vital and Health Statistics Subcommittee on Populations Workshop on Data Linkages to Improve Health Outcomes, Washington, D.C., September 18, 2006.

Pudney, Stephen, *Modelling Individual Choice: The Econometrics of Corners, Kinks, and Holes,* Oxford: Basil, 1989.

Ringel, Jeannie, and Jacob Alex Klerman, *Today or Last Year? How Do Interviewees Answer the CPS Health Insurance Questions?* Santa Monica, Calif.: RAND Corporation, WR-288, 2005. As of August 22, 2007:
http://www.rand.org/pubs/working_papers/WR288/

Roos, Cpl. Joe, and Sgt. Daryl Sanford, "At Last! They're Home," Minnesota National Guard Web site, July 20, 2007. As of May 16, 2008:
http://www.minnesotanationalguard.org/press_room/e-zine/articles/index.php?item=875

Stafford, Frank, "Forestalling the Demise of Empirical Economics: The Role of Microdata in Labor Economics Research," in *Handbook of Labor Economics*, 1st ed., Orley Ashenfelter and Richard Layard, eds., Amsterdam, N.Y.: North-Holland, 1986, pp. 387–423.

Stock, James H., and Mark W. Watson, *Introduction to Econometrics*, Boston, Mass.: Addison-Wesley, 2003.

Tourangeau, Roger, Lance J. Rips, and Kenneth Rasinski, *The Psychology of Survey Response,* Cambridge, UK: Cambridge University Press, 2000.

U.S. Bureau of Labor Statistics, "National Longitudinal Surveys," undated. As of July 27, 2007:
http://www.bls.gov/nls/

U.S. Census Bureau, "Census 2000: Plans and Rules for Taking the Census—Residence Rules," last revised April 25, 2003. As of July 27, 2007:
http://www.census.gov/population/www/censusdata/resid_rules.html

———, "NLSY79 User's Guide: A Guide to the 1979–2002 National Longitudinal Survey of Youth Data," Ohio State University, Columbus, Ohio, January 2004. As of July 27, 2007:
http://www.bls.gov/nls/79guide/nls79usg.htm

U.S. Department of Defense, "The Millennium Cohort Study," Web site, undated. As of May 5, 2008:
http://www.millenniumcohort.org/

U.S. Office of Management and Budget, *Questions and Answers When Designing Surveys for Information Collections*, Washington, D.C.: Office of Regulatory Affairs, Office of Management and Budget, January 2006a. As of August 17, 2007:
http://www.whitehouse.gov/omb/inforeg/pmc_survey_guidance_2006.pdf

———, "Standards and Guidelines for Statistical Surveys," Washington, D.C.: White House, September 2006b. As of August 13, 2007:
http://www.whitehouse.gov/omb/inforeg/statpolicy/standards_stat_surveys.pdf

Verbeek, Marno, and Theo Nijman, "Minimum MSE Estimation of a Regression Model with Fixed Effects from a Series of Cross Sections," *Journal of Econometrics*, Vol. 59, Nos. 1–2, September 1993, pp. 125–136.

Weinberg, Daniel H., Charles T. Nelson, Marc I. Roemer, and Edward J. Welniak Jr., "Fifty Years of U.S. Income Data from the Current Population Survey: Alternatives, Trends, and Quality," *The American Economic Review*, Vol. 89, No. 2, May 1999, pp. 18–22.

Warner, John T., Curtis J. Simon, and Deborah M. Payne, "The Military Recruiting Productivity Slowdown: The Roles of Resources, Opportunity Cost and the Tastes of Youth," *Defence and Peace Economics*, Vol. 14, No. 5, October 2003.